"Nurturing Self-Care:

Empowering Resilience through Life's Challenges."

By Dr. Tracy A. Allen

# Nurturing Self-Care

*Empowering Resilience Through Life's Challenges*

By

Dr. T. A Allen

# Dedication

To my beloved children, Jerome A. Johnson II and Travis Boaz Johnson,

I dedicate this to you both, acknowledging the incredible men you have become. Your strength, character, and integrity are a testament to the love and values instilled in you. I am endlessly proud of the paths you are forging and your impact on this world.

I owe everything to God, my unwavering foundation and constant throughout my life. I attribute all I am, all I have, and all I will ever be to Your divine plan and grace. You have given me a voice, talents, and life experiences, both joyous and challenging, each playing a crucial part in shaping the person I am today. For Your guidance, protection, and love, I am eternally grateful.

With all my heart, thank you, God.

Dear Valued Readers,

I am thrilled to announce the release of this book, a work that embodies not just my insights and experiences but also the collective wisdom of a journey shared by life challenges. This book is a testament to the belief that within each of us lies the potential for tremendous growth, understanding, and transformation.

As you turn each page, I invite you to embark on a journey of exploration, discovery, and self-reflection with me. This book is more than just a collection of words; it is a conversation that helps you to relate, connect, and grow.

Your support and engagement mean the world to me. It is for you that these words have been penned with the hope that they will resonate with your experiences, challenges, and aspirations. I desire this book to be a source of inspiration, a beacon of hope, and a guide in your journey toward fulfillment and well-being.

I am incredibly grateful for the opportunity to share this part of myself with you and eagerly await the moments when our paths intersect through the pages of this book. Your presence in this journey enriches it, adding depth and meaning to every word.

Thank you for being a part of this adventure. I look forward to the conversations and connections that will emerge as you delve into the chapters of this book. Here's to the journey ahead, filled with learning, growth, and shared experiences.

Warm regards,

# TABLE OF CONTENTS

**Chapter 1: Understanding the Importance of Self-Care**

Recognizing the Significance of Self-Care in Promoting Overall Well-Being

Exploring the Connection Between Self-Care and Resilience in Coping with Life's **Challenges**

**Chapter 2: Unraveling PTSD and Self-Care Strategies**

Understanding Post-Traumatic Stress Disorder (PTSD) and Common Triggers

Practical Self-Care Techniques to Manage PTSD Symptoms and Promote Healing

**Chapter 3: Mental Health and Self-Care**

Shining a Light on Mental Health Challenges and Their Impact on Well-Being

Identifying Self-Care Practices that Support Mental Well-Being and Emotional Balance

**Chapter 4: Embracing Self-Care through the Cancer Journey**

Navigating the Difficult Terrain of a Cancer Diagnosis and Treatment

Empowering self-care Strategies to Enhance Physical, Emotional, and Spiritual Resilience

**Chapter 5: Divorce: Rebuilding through Self-Care**

Coping with the Emotional Aftermath of Divorce and the Challenges it Brings

Promoting Self-Care Practices that Foster Healing, Self-Discovery, and Personal Growth

**Chapter 6: The Importance of Boundaries in Self-Care**

Understanding the Role of Boundaries in Protecting One's Well-Being

Establishing and Maintaining Healthy Boundaries in Various Aspects of Life

**Chapter 7: Building a Supportive Network in Self-Care**

Recognizing the Significance of Social Support in Times of Adversity

Strategies to Cultivate Meaningful Relationships and Seek Support During Challenging Life Transitions

## Chapter 8: Mindfulness and Self-Care

Exploring the benefits of mindfulness in promoting self-awareness and resilience

Integrating mindfulness techniques into daily self-care routines

## Chapter 9: Nurturing Physical Self-Care

The Impact of Physical Well-Being on Overall Mental and Emotional Health

Incorporating Physical Self-care Practices into Daily Life to Promote Restoration and Vitality

## Chapter 10: Crafting Emotional Self-Care Rituals

The Necessity of Nurturing Emotional Well-Being During Times of Adversity

Self-Care Practices that Foster Emotional Growth, Self-Compassion, and Resilience

## Chapter 11: Finding Meaning and Purpose in Self-Care

Rediscovering Personal Values and Passions through Introspection

Cultivating Self-Care Practices that Align with One's Purpose and Enable Personal Growth

## Chapter 12: Sustaining Self-Care for Long-Term Well-Being

Strategies for Maintaining Self-care Routines and Preventing Burnout

Nurturing Resilience to Navigate Future Challenges with Strength and Self-Compassion

# Epilogue

## Nurturing Self-Care: A Lifelong Companion

Nurturing Self-Care is not just a book; it's a lifelong companion on your journey to well-being. This comprehensive guide offers practical advice, tools, and insights to individuals seeking to enhance their well-being while dealing with significant life challenges such as PTSD, mental health issues, cancer, or divorce. It's packed with practical advice and actionable strategies you can use today. Self-care is a powerful tool for enhancing overall well-being. This book provides practical advice and actionable strategies, empowering you to effectively incorporate self-care into your daily routine and prepare for a healthier and more fulfilling life. Life is filled with challenges, and developing resilience is critical to navigating these obstacles with strength and grace. Through self-care practices, readers will learn how to build resilience by nurturing their inner strength and cultivating a positive mindset. This resilience will help you face life's difficulties and empower you to conquer them confidently and persevere.

For those dealing with PTSD, mental health issues, or cancer, self-care can play a crucial role in the healing process. This book recognizes that emotional well-being is a critical component of overall health and offers specific practices and techniques tailored to these unique challenges, helping you to manage symptoms, reduce stress, and promote overall healing. By addressing these conditions' physical and emotional aspects, self-care can significantly enhance your quality of life. Nurturing Self-Care provides tools and strategies to help you process difficult emotions, build emotional resilience, and develop a deeper understanding of your emotional needs. Whether coping with the aftermath of a divorce or managing chronic stress, this book offers valuable insights to support and validate your emotional well-being.

Self-care is not just about maintaining your current well-being; it is also about personal growth and self-discovery. The practices and exercises outlined in this book encourage readers to explore their values, passions, and goals. This journey of self-discovery can lead to greater self-awareness and a more profound understanding of what brings you joy and fulfillment. The journey to well-being is a lifelong process. Nurturing Self-Care encourages readers to remain open to new experiences and continuous learning. By staying curious and embracing new self-care practices, you can continue to evolve and grow throughout your life. This book serves as a guide to help you navigate this ongoing journey with confidence and curiosity.

Self-care is most effective when supported by firm friends, family, and community networks. This book emphasizes building and maintaining supportive relationships, encouraging accountability and emotional support. Fostering these connections creates a supportive environment that enhances self-care efforts.

In addition to personal and social support, professional help can be an invaluable resource on your self-care journey. Nurturing Self-Care highlights the importance of seeking therapy, counseling, or other professional services when needed. These resources can provide specialized guidance and support, helping you to overcome challenges and achieve your well-being goals.

The journey to enhanced well-being begins with a single step. This book calls on you to take that step today. Whether incorporating a new self-care practice into your routine, reaching out for support, or simply taking a moment to reflect on your needs, every action brings you closer to a healthier, more fulfilling life. Committing to self-care is a powerful declaration of your worth and desire to live a balanced, joyful life. Nurturing Self-Care invites you to commit wholeheartedly, knowing it is an investment in your present and future well-being.

As you conclude your reading of Nurturing Self-Care, may you move forward with renewed confidence and determination. This book is your guide, companion, and source of inspiration on the path to well-being. Embrace the journey, celebrate your progress, and always remember the importance of nurturing yourself. Your well-being is a priority, and this book reminds you of that.

Through self-care practices, readers will be encouraged to foster resilience, promote healing, and embark on personal growth and self-discovery. Nurturing Self-Care is a beacon of hope and a roadmap to a life filled with balance, happiness, and well-being. Your journey is unique, and this book is here to support you every step of the way. Celebrate your progress, and always remember the importance of nurturing yourself. Wishing you continued growth, resilience, and fulfillment as you nurture yourself and thrive in all aspects of life.

# Introduction

We often run on empty in life's relentless demands, challenges, and uncertainties. The modern world, with its constant stream of responsibilities and distractions, can leave us feeling overwhelmed, disconnected, and mentally exhausted. In our pursuit of success, happiness, and fulfillment, we sometimes forget the most crucial aspect of our journey: taking care of ourselves.

Welcome to "Nurturing Self-Care: Empowering Resilience through Life's Challenges." In these pages, we embark on a profound exploration of the art and science of self-care. This journey promises to rejuvenate your spirit and empower you with the resilience to weather life's storms.

Self-care is more than just a buzzword or a fleeting trend. It is a fundamental pillar of our well-being, a source of strength, and a pathway to personal growth. It is the intentional act of nourishing our physical, emotional, mental, social, and spiritual needs. It's about recognizing that we must first care for ourselves to thrive.

## What Self-Care Truly Means

In this book, we will delve deep into the essence of self-care—what it truly means and how it can transform our lives. We will dispel common myths and misconceptions, uncover the various dimensions of self-care, and explore the profound connection between self-care and resilience.

### The Multifaceted Nature of Self-Care

Self-care encompasses various aspects of our lives. It includes:

- ➤ Physical Self-Care: Activities that improve physical health, such as exercise, nutrition, and sleep.
- ➤ Emotional Self-Care: Practices that help us process and manage our emotions, like journaling, therapy, and mindfulness.
- ➤ Mental Self-Care: Engaging in activities stimulating and challenging our minds, such as reading, learning, and creative pursuits.
- ➤ Social Self-Care: Building and maintaining healthy relationships and social connections.
- ➤ Spiritual Self-Care: Practices that nurture our spirit and provide a sense of purpose and meaning.

# The Connection Between Self-Care and Resilience

Resilience, the ability to bounce back from adversity and thrive despite life's challenges, is not an innate trait reserved for the chosen few. It is a skill that can be developed and honed through self-care practices. By nurturing self-care, you will equip yourself with the tools and mindset to face life's inevitable ups and downs with strength, grace, and unwavering determination.

## Building Resilience Through Self-Care

Throughout these chapters, we will journey together through the foundations of self-care, from self-awareness to setting boundaries and prioritizing your well-being. We will explore the physical, emotional, mental, social, spiritual, and creative aspects of self-care, providing you with practical strategies and actionable steps to weave self-care into the fabric of your daily life. Resilience significantly impacts our overall well-being. It enables us to manage stress, recover from setbacks, and maintain a positive outlook even in difficult times. Integrating self-care into our lives strengthens our resilience and enhances our capacity to thrive. Life's challenges are an inescapable part of the human experience. From stress and anxiety to grief and illness, we will face our share of trials. Yet, by embracing self-care as a lifelong practice, we can weather these storms and emerge from them more robust, wiser, and more resilient than ever before.

This book is a roadmap—a guide to nurturing self-care and unlocking the resilience that lies within you. It is an invitation to prioritize your well-being, to celebrate your progress, and to inspire others on their journeys of self-discovery and empowerment. Embracing self-care is a journey of self-discovery and empowerment. Exploring the various dimensions of self-care will uncover more profound insights into your needs, values, and aspirations. This journey will enhance your well-being and empower you to live a more authentic and fulfilling life.

## An Invitation to Transform Your Life

So, let's embark on this transformative journey together. Let's explore the transformative power of self-care and uncover the keys to empowered resilience. Your path to a more vibrant, resilient, and fulfilling life begins here. Committing to self-care is a powerful declaration of your worth and desire to live a balanced, joyful life. This book invites you to commit wholeheartedly, knowing it is an investment in your present and future well-being.

**Celebrating Progress**

As you progress on this journey, take time to celebrate your achievements. Every step you take towards better self-care is a victory. Recognize and honor the positive changes you make in your life.

**My Final Thoughts**

Nurturing self-care will foster resilience, promote healing, and embark on personal growth and self-discovery. This book is a beacon of hope and a guide to a balance, happiness, and well-being-filled life. May you continue to flourish and thrive in all areas of your life, always remembering the importance of nurturing yourself. Your self-care journey is a beautiful testament to your commitment to living a life of balance and happiness.

**Welcome to "Nurturing Self-Care: Empowering Resilience through Life's Challenges." Your journey towards a more vibrant, resilient, and fulfilling life starts now.**

**"Nurturing Self-Care:**

**Empowering Resilience through Life's Challenges."**

## Chapter 1: Recognizing the Significance of Self-Care

In this chapter, we will explore the vital role of self-care in nurturing our overall well-being. Self-care is more than pampering oneself or indulging in occasional treats—it is an essential practice that empowers us to navigate life's challenges with resilience and strength. We live in a fast-paced, demanding world where our physical, mental, and emotional well-being can often be overlooked. Daily life's constant hustle and bustle can leave us feeling drained and disconnected from ourselves. Amidst these demands, self-care is a gentle reminder to prioritize our needs and take intentional actions to nurture our holistic health. It is about carving out time to recharge and reconnect with our inner selves, allowing us to maintain balance and harmony.

**Beyond Surface-Level Pampering**

Recognizing the significance of self-care goes beyond surface-level pampering. It involves understanding that when we prioritize our well-being, we become better equipped to handle the ups and downs that life throws our way. It is like putting on your oxygen mask before helping others—it enables us to show up as our best selves for others. By engaging in self-care practices, we cultivate a deeper connection with ourselves, enhancing our ability to support and care for those around us. This deeper connection fosters self-awareness and emotional intelligence, helping us navigate relationships and challenges more effectively.

**Cultivating Connection and Setting Boundaries**

Through self-care practices, we cultivate a deeper connection with ourselves, allowing us to understand our needs better and set healthier boundaries. This connection helps us recognize when to step back and recharge, preventing burnout and exhaustion. By nourishing our mind, body, and spirit, we replenish our inner resources, fostering resilience and fortitude in adversity. Self-care empowers us to say no when necessary, protecting our energy and well-being. It also encourages us to seek support and help, reminding us that we don't have to face challenges alone.

**Research on Self-Care and Its Benefits**

Research has shown that engaging in regular self-care activities reduces stress, anxiety, and burnout. It enhances our capacity to cope with stressors, improves emotional regulation, and promotes a positive outlook. By taking time for self-care, we can manage our stress levels more effectively, improving mental health and overall well-being. Self-care is an act of self-love and a self-compassionate way to honor and care for ourselves holistically and sustainably. It is about recognizing our worth and valuing ourselves enough to prioritize our health and happiness.

## The Personal Nature of Self-Care

Furthermore, self-care is not a one-size-fits-all approach. It is deeply personal and varies from person to person. What works for one individual may not work for another. It is about discovering what brings you joy, peace, and rejuvenation. This personal nature of self-care encourages us to explore different practices and find what resonates with us. It might be a morning meditation, a walk in nature, a creative hobby, or simply taking a few moments of quiet solitude. The key is to listen to our inner voice and honor our unique needs.

## Exploring Various Self-Care Strategies

Throughout this book, we will explore various self-care strategies that can be tailored to your unique circumstances and preferences. There is a wide range of self-care options, from mindfulness practices to physical activities and creative pursuits to relaxation techniques. By recognizing the significance of self-care and its connection to resilience, you are taking the first step towards empowering yourself to navigate life's challenges with greater ease and grace. Each strategy we explore will offer practical tips and insights to help you integrate self-care into your daily routine.

## Self-Care as an Investment in Well-Being

Remember, self-care is not selfish but an investment in your well-being. By taking care of yourself, you are ensuring you have the energy and capacity to take care of others and fulfill your responsibilities. It is about creating a sustainable practice that supports your long-term health and happiness. Self-care is honoring yourself and acknowledging that you deserve to be cared for and nurtured.

## Embarking on the Journey Together

So, let us embark on this journey together as we discover the transformative power of self-care in nurturing resilience and promoting overall well-being. As we move forward, keep an open mind and heart and be willing to explore and experiment with different self-care practices. The journey to self-care is a personal and evolving process, and there is no right or wrong way to do it. The important thing is to start and make self-care a priority in your life.

By embracing self-care, you take a proactive step towards a healthier, more balanced, and fulfilling life. Together, we will explore the many facets of self-care and uncover the practices that resonate with you. Let's begin this journey of self-discovery and well-being and unlock the potential for a more resilient and empowered you.

## Chapter 2: Understanding PTSD and Self-Care Strategies

In this chapter, we will explore post-traumatic stress disorder (PTSD) and how self-care practices can support individuals in managing their symptoms and promoting healing. PTSD is a complex mental health condition that can develop after experiencing or witnessing a traumatic event. It can manifest in various ways and significantly impact an individual's daily life.

Understanding PTSD is crucial to addressing its symptoms and providing appropriate support effectively. Traumatic events such as accidents, natural disasters, combat experiences, or personal assaults can trigger the development of PTSD. These events can leave lasting impressions on the mind, leading to various symptoms. Common symptoms may include intrusive thoughts, nightmares, hypervigilance, emotional numbness, and avoidance of triggers associated with the traumatic event. These symptoms can severely disrupt daily functioning, affecting work, relationships, and overall quality of life.

Intrusive thoughts are recurrent, unwanted memories of the traumatic event that can surface unexpectedly, causing significant distress. Trauma reminders, such as certain sounds, smells, or situations, can trigger these thoughts. Nightmares, on the other hand, are distressing dreams related to traumatic events. These nightmares can be so vivid and terrifying that they disrupt sleep, leading to insomnia and further exacerbating PTSD symptoms.

Hypervigilance refers to a state of heightened alertness and constant scanning of the environment for potential threats. It can result in a persistent feeling of being on edge, making it difficult to relax or feel safe. Emotional numbness is another common symptom of PTSD, where individuals may feel detached from their emotions or the world around them. It can lead to difficulties connecting with others and experiencing joy or pleasure.

Avoidance is a coping mechanism often employed by individuals with PTSD. They may avoid places, people, or activities that remind them of the traumatic event. While this can provide temporary relief, it can also lead to isolation and prevent individuals from fully engaging in life. Avoidance can also reinforce the fear associated with trauma, making it harder to confront and process traumatic memories.

# The Role of Self-Care in Managing PTSD

Practicing self-care is vital for individuals coping with PTSD, as it provides them with tools to soothe distressing symptoms and facilitate healing. While self-care alone may not treat the underlying condition, it can aid in managing symptoms and promoting well-being. Self-care helps create a supportive environment that fosters emotional and physical healing, empowering individuals to regain control over their lives.

The self-care strategies discussed in this chapter will focus on creating a safe and nurturing environment, fostering emotional regulation, and cultivating a sense of empowerment. By engaging in self-care practices, individuals can develop a stronger sense of control over their lives and reduce the impact of PTSD on their overall well-being. A calm physical environment can be achieved through relaxing activities like aromatherapy, visualization exercises, or a comforting self-care space. These practices can help individuals find solace and create a sense of safety.

Emotional self-care is also essential in navigating PTSD symptoms. Techniques such as journaling, art therapy, mindfulness, and deep breathing exercises can help individuals regulate their emotions, process traumatic experiences, and reduce anxiety and stress. Journaling allows for expressing thoughts and feelings, providing a safe outlet for processing emotions. Art therapy encourages creative expression, which can be therapeutic and healing. Mindfulness practices, such as meditation and deep breathing exercises, help ground individuals in the present moment, reducing anxiety and promoting relaxation.

## Physical Self-Care and Routine

Additionally, establishing a consistent self-care routine that includes regular exercise, healthy eating, and sufficient rest can significantly impact one's physical and emotional well-being. Physical activity releases endorphins, natural mood enhancers, and helps reduce stress and anxiety. A balanced diet provides the necessary nutrients to support brain and body function, while adequate rest is crucial for overall health and recovery. Engaging in activities that bring joy and give a sense of purpose, such as hobbies, socializing, or volunteering, also plays a crucial role in managing symptoms and fostering healing.

It is important to remember that self-care strategies for PTSD may differ for each individual, and customization is key. What works well for one person may not necessarily work for another. The key is to explore various techniques, remain patient and compassionate with oneself, and seek professional support when needed. Therapists and support groups can provide additional guidance and support, helping individuals develop personalized self-care plans.

### Seeking Professional Support

Professional support is often essential for individuals with PTSD. Trauma-trained therapists can offer specialized treatment approaches, such as cognitive-behavioral therapy (CBT), eye movement desensitization and reprocessing (EMDR), and other evidence-based therapies. These treatments can help individuals process traumatic memories, reduce symptoms, and develop healthier coping mechanisms. Support groups can also provide a sense of community and understanding, allowing individuals to share their experiences and learn from others facing similar challenges.

By incorporating self-care strategies into their lives, individuals with PTSD can take significant steps towards managing symptoms, promoting healing, and gradually regaining control over their lives. In the following chapters, we will delve further into self-care practices tailored to other challenging life experiences, including mental health, cancer, and divorce. Each chapter will offer insights and practical tips to help you navigate these experiences with resilience and self-compassion.

## A Journey of Healing and Empowerment

Remember, healing from PTSD is a personal and unique process. It requires patience, self-compassion, and a willingness to explore different strategies. By prioritizing self-care, you are taking an active role in your healing journey and empowering yourself to overcome the challenges associated with PTSD. Together, we will explore the transformative power of self-care and its ability to foster resilience, promote well-being, and create a life filled with hope and possibility.

# Chapter 3: Nurturing Mental Health and Self-Care

This chapter will illuminate mental health challenges and their profound impact on well-being. We will explore the importance of prioritizing mental health and identify self-care practices that support emotional balance and promote mental well-being. Mental health is essential to our overall health, yet it is often stigmatized and overlooked. It is vital to understand that mental health challenges can affect anyone, regardless of age, gender, or background. From stress and anxiety to depression and other mood disorders, mental health challenges can significantly impact our daily lives and overall quality of life. Mental health is not just the absence of mental illness but a state of well-being in which an individual realizes their potential, can cope with the everyday stresses of life, work productively, and contribute to their community.

## Breaking the Silence

We break the silence and encourage open dialogue about mental health by acknowledging and shining a light on these challenges. Mental health stigma can prevent individuals from seeking the help they need, leading to a worsening of symptoms and a reduced quality of life. This chapter aims to provide insights and practical tools to nurture mental well-being through self-care practices. We can create a more inclusive and understanding society by fostering an environment where mental health is openly discussed and supported.

## Understanding Mental Health Challenges

Mental health challenges can manifest in various forms, each affecting individuals differently. Understanding these challenges is the first step toward effective self-care and support.

- ➢ **Stress and Anxiety**-Stress and anxiety are common mental health challenges that many people experience. Stress is the body's response to perceived threats or pressures, while anxiety is a feeling of worry or fear about future events. Both can lead to physical symptoms such as headaches, muscle tension, fatigue and emotional symptoms like irritability, restlessness, and difficulty concentrating.
- ➢ **Depression and Mood Disorders**- Depression is a mood disorder characterized by persistent feelings of sadness, hopelessness, and a lack of interest or pleasure in activities. It can affect one's ability to function daily and may lead to physical symptoms like changes in

appetite and sleep patterns. Other mood disorders, such as bipolar disorder, involve fluctuations in mood from extreme highs (mania) to extreme lows (depression).

**Other Mental Health Conditions**

Other mental health conditions include post-traumatic stress disorder (PTSD), obsessive-compulsive disorder (OCD), and schizophrenia. Each condition has its symptoms and requires tailored self-care and treatment approaches. Understanding the diversity of mental health challenges is essential for appropriate support and care.

**Self-Care Practices for Mental Well-Being**

Self-care practices that support mental well-being involve intentional actions and strategies to improve emotional balance. These practices are beneficial not only for those with mental health challenges but also for anyone looking to maintain or enhance their mental health.

### 1. Self-Reflection and Awareness

Self-reflection and awareness are foundational elements of mental well-being. Journaling, meditation, and mindfulness exercises can enhance self-awareness and help individuals identify their emotional needs and triggers. Journaling provides a safe space to express thoughts and feelings, allowing for better understanding and processing of emotions. Meditation and mindfulness exercises promote present-moment awareness, reducing stress and enhancing emotional regulation.

### 2. Emotional Regulation Techniques

Learning and practicing techniques like deep breathing, progressive muscle relaxation, and grounding exercises can support individuals in managing and regulating their emotions more effectively. Deep breathing exercises can calm the nervous system and reduce stress. Progressive muscle relaxation involves tensing and relaxing different muscle groups, promoting physical and emotional relaxation. Grounding exercises, is as focusing on the senses or engaging in physical activity, help bring attention to the present moment and reduce anxiety.

### 3. Seeking Professional Support

Recognizing the importance of seeking professional help is crucial for mental well-being. Connecting with a therapist or counselor can offer guidance, validation, and tools to navigate mental health challenges. Professional support can provide structured treatment plans tailored to individual needs, such as cognitive-behavioral therapy (CBT) or medication management.

### 4. Establishing Healthy Boundaries

Setting clear boundaries and learning to say no when necessary is crucial for protecting one's mental health and maintaining emotional balance. Healthy boundaries involve recognizing one's limits and communicating them effectively to others. It can prevent burnout, reduce stress, and improve relationships by fostering mutual respect and understanding.

### 5. Engaging in Creative Outlets

Art therapy, music, dance, or creative expression can be powerful self-care tools, allowing individuals to process emotions, release stress, and promote mental well-being. Creative activities provide an outlet for self-expression and can be a source of joy and fulfillment. Engaging in creative pursuits can also enhance cognitive function and give a sense of accomplishment.

### 6. Building Healthy Relationships

Cultivating supportive relationships and meaningful connections with others can enhance mental well-being by providing a sense of belonging, support, and understanding. Healthy relationships involve mutual respect, trust, and effective communication. Social support can buffer against stress and provide emotional resources during challenging times.

### 7. Taking Time for Rest

Practicing self-care through restful activities like getting enough sleep, taking breaks, engaging in hobbies, and prioritizing leisure time can rejuvenate the mind and promote mental well-being. Rest is essential for physical and psychological recovery, and sufficient sleep is crucial for cognitive function and emotional regulation. Taking breaks and engaging in enjoyable activities can prevent burnout and promote overall health.

## The Ongoing Practice of Self-Care

Remember that self-care is not a one-time event but an ongoing practice that requires regular attention and care. It is essential to tailor self-care methods to individual needs and preferences. Each person's self-care journey is unique, so exploring different techniques and determining what works best for you is crucial. Self-care should be flexible and adaptable, evolving with changing needs and circumstances.

**Customizing Self-Care Strategies**

Customization is critical in self-care. What works for one person may not work for another. Being patient and compassionate with oneself is essential while exploring different self-care practices. Regularly reassessing and adjusting self-care routines can ensure they remain effective and aligned with personal needs.

**Seeking Support and Resources**

In addition to personal self-care practices, seeking support and resources from community organizations, support groups, and mental health professionals can enhance well-being. Many communities offer resources such as hotlines, workshops, and online forums that provide information and support for mental health. Integrating self-care practices that support mental well-being into daily life can enhance emotional balance, build resiliency, and create a foundation for long-lasting mental health. Making self-care a daily habit can lead to sustained improvements in mental health and overall quality of life. Simple actions, such as taking a few minutes daily for mindfulness or ensuring regular social interactions, can make a significant difference.

**Creating a Self-Care Plan**

Creating a self-care plan can help individuals prioritize and structure their self-care activities. A self-care plan might include various practices, such as scheduling regular exercise, setting aside time for hobbies, and planning regular check-ins with a therapist. By having a plan, individuals can ensure they are consistently engaging in activities that support their mental health.

**Adapting to Life Changes**

Life changes and unexpected challenges can impact mental health and self-care routines. Adaptability and willingness to adjust self-care practices in response to life changes are essential. It might involve seeking additional support during stressful periods or modifying routines to accommodate new responsibilities.

**Moving Forward**

In the following chapters, we will further explore self-care approaches tailored to challenging life experiences such as dealing with cancer and divorce, where mental well-being is of utmost importance. Each chapter will provide insights and practical tips to help navigate these experiences with resilience and self-compassion. By prioritizing self-care, individuals can build a strong foundation for mental health that supports them through life's challenges.

**Commitment to Self-Care**

A commitment to self-care is a commitment to one's health and well-being. It is an ongoing journey that requires dedication and self-compassion. By prioritizing self-care, individuals can enhance their mental health, improve their quality of life, and build resilience against future challenges. Together, we will explore the transformative power of self-care and its ability to nurture mental well-being and create a life filled with balance, purpose, and joy.

# Chapter 4: Embracing Self-Care through the Cancer Journey

In this chapter, we will explore the challenging terrain of a cancer diagnosis and treatment and the decisive role that self-care can play in enhancing physical, emotional, and spiritual resilience during this challenging journey.

## The Impact of a Cancer Diagnosis

Receiving a cancer diagnosis can be an overwhelming and life-altering experience. It can bring forth a wide range of emotions, including fear, anxiety, and uncertainty. During this time, it is crucial to prioritize self-care to nurture oneself holistically and promote a sense of empowerment and resilience. The journey through cancer is not just a physical battle but an emotional and spiritual one as well. Understanding the multifaceted impact of cancer can help in developing a comprehensive self-care strategy.

## Emotional Repercussions

The emotional impact of a cancer diagnosis cannot be overstated. Patients often experience a whirlwind of emotions, ranging from shock and denial to anger, sadness, and fear. These emotions can be triggered by concerns about the future, potential changes in physical appearance, and the stress of undergoing treatment. It's important to acknowledge and address these emotions rather than suppress them.

## Physical Challenges

Cancer and its treatments can lead to a variety of physical challenges, including fatigue, pain, nausea, and changes in appetite. These symptoms can affect daily functioning and overall quality of life. Managing these physical symptoms is a crucial aspect of self-care.

## Spiritual and Existential Questions

A cancer diagnosis can also prompt deep existential and spiritual questions. Patients may question life's meaning, faith, and purpose. Addressing these spiritual concerns is an essential component of holistic self-care.

## Self-Care Strategies for Physical Well-Being

Self-care strategies can make a significant difference in navigating the cancer journey. They provide practical tools for managing physical symptoms and side effects and support emotional well-being and spiritual growth.

## Healthy Eating and Nutrition

One essential aspect of self-care during the cancer journey is prioritizing physical well-being. It can include healthy eating and a balanced diet to support the body's healing process. Consuming nutrient-rich foods can help maintain strength and energy levels. Some specific dietary tips include:

- **High-Protein Foods**: Protein is essential for repairing tissues and maintaining muscle mass. Including lean meats, eggs, dairy products, and plant-based proteins can be beneficial.
- **Fruits and Vegetables:** These provide essential vitamins, minerals, and antioxidants to support the immune system and overall health.
- **Hydration:** Staying hydrated is crucial, especially if experiencing side effects like vomiting or diarrhea.

## Gentle Exercise

Doing gentle exercises like yoga or walking can improve energy levels and enhance overall physical resilience. Exercise can also help reduce fatigue, improve mood, and enhance sleep quality. Tailoring exercise routines to individual energy levels and physical capabilities is essential. Some recommended activities include:

- **Walking**: A low-impact exercise that can be adjusted to individual fitness levels.
- **Yoga:** Helps improve flexibility, strength, and relaxation.
- **Swimming:** Provides a full-body workout with minimal strain on the joints.

## Rest and Sleep

Incorporating rest and sleep into daily routines is vital for the body's rejuvenation and healing. Quality sleep can enhance immune function, mood, and cognitive performance. Creating a restful sleep environment and establishing a regular sleep schedule can support better sleep. Tips for improving sleep include:

- **Consistent Sleep Schedule:** Going to bed and waking up simultaneously every day.

- ➤ **Sleep Environment:** Ensuring the bedroom is dark, quiet, and calm.
- ➤ **Relaxation Techniques**: Deep breathing, meditation, or reading practices can help signal the body that it's time to wind down.

## Emotional Self-Care

Emotional self-care is equally important. Cancer can evoke a rollercoaster of emotions, including sadness, anger, and anxiety. Finding healthy outlets for feelings, such as talking to a therapist, joining support groups, or expressing oneself through creative activities like journaling or art therapy, can provide emotional relief and promote healing.

## Therapy and Counseling

Talking to a therapist or counselor can provide a safe space to process emotions, receive validation, and develop coping strategies. Therapy can help individuals navigate the emotional complexities of a cancer diagnosis and treatment. Some therapeutic approaches include:

- ➤ **Cognitive Behavioral Therapy (CBT):** Helps identify and change negative thought patterns.
- ➤ **Supportive Counseling:** Provides emotional support and validation.
- ➤ **Group Therapy**: Offers a sense of community and shared experience.

## Support Groups

Joining support groups can create a sense of community and provide emotional support from others who are going through similar experiences. These groups can offer a platform for sharing experiences, advice, and encouragement.

## Creative Outlets

Expressing oneself through creative activities like journaling, art therapy, music, or dance can be a powerful way to process emotions and reduce stress. These activities can provide a sense of accomplishment and joy, helping to counterbalance the emotional toll of cancer.

## Spiritual Self-Care

Spiritual self-care plays a significant role in nurturing resilience as well. Cancer can challenge one's faith, beliefs, and sense of purpose. Engaging in activities promoting spiritual well-being, such as meditation, prayer, or connecting with a supportive community, can bring peace, meaning, and hope during the challenging moments of the cancer journey.

**Meditation and Mindfulness**

Meditation and mindfulness can help individuals stay grounded and present, reducing anxiety and promoting peace. These practices can also enhance emotional regulation and provide a space for reflection and spiritual connection.

**Prayer and Faith-Based Activities**

Prayer and other faith-based activities can provide solace and strength for those who find comfort in their faith. These might include attending religious services, reading spiritual texts, or participating in community worship.

**Connecting with a Supportive Community**

Building connections with a supportive spiritual community can provide a sense of belonging and shared purpose. This community can offer emotional support, spiritual guidance, and a network of care.

**Building a Supportive Social Network**

Self-care practices during the cancer journey go beyond the individual. A supportive social network can provide a lifeline of comfort and understanding. Building connections with loved ones, seeking support from healthcare professionals, and joining cancer support groups can create a sense of belonging and emotional help.

- **Support from Loved Ones-** Loved ones can provide practical support, emotional encouragement, and a sense of normalcy. Open communication with family and friends about needs and feelings can strengthen these relationships and enhance support.
- **Professional Support**- Healthcare professionals, including doctors, nurses, and social workers, can offer medical care, emotional support, and resources for coping with cancer. Developing a solid relationship with the healthcare team can ensure comprehensive care and support.
- **Cancer Support Groups**- Joining cancer support groups can provide a sense of community and shared experience. These groups can offer practical advice, emotional support, and encouragement from others who understand the challenges of the cancer journey.
- **Empowering Oneself through Knowledge-** Empowering oneself through knowledge is another crucial aspect of self-care during the cancer journey. Educating oneself about the diagnosis, treatment

options, and coping mechanisms can help individuals make informed decisions and actively participate in their healthcare journey.

**Researching the Diagnosis**

Understanding the specific type of cancer, its progression, and treatment options can provide a sense of control and preparedness. Reliable sources of information include medical websites, books, and discussions with healthcare providers.

**Exploring Treatment Options**

Exploring various treatment options, including their benefits, risks, and potential side effects, can help individuals make informed decisions. It might include conventional treatments like chemotherapy and radiation, as well as complementary therapies like acupuncture and nutrition counseling.

**Learning Coping Mechanisms**

Learning about coping mechanisms for managing the physical and emotional challenges of cancer can enhance resilience and well-being. It might include stress management techniques, relaxation exercises, and lifestyle modifications.

## Moving Forward with Self-Care

By embracing self-care strategies throughout the cancer journey, individuals can enhance their overall well-being, cope with treatment side effects, and foster emotional and spiritual resilience. Self-care becomes an act of self-empowerment, allowing individuals to navigate the rugged terrain of cancer with grace, strength, and hope.

**Integrating Self-Care into Daily Life**

Integrating self-care into daily routines can ensure these practices become a consistent part of life. It might involve setting aside time daily for self-care activities, creating a supportive environment, and regularly reassessing self-care needs and strategies.

**Continuing the Journey**

In the subsequent chapters, we will explore self-care approaches that can guide individuals through other challenging life experiences, such as divorce and coping with mental health challenges. These chapters offer support and tools to navigate these journeys with resilience and care.

Individuals can build a strong foundation for overall well-being and resilience by continuing to prioritize self-care.

# Chapter 5: Divorce: Rebuilding through Self-Care

In this chapter, we will delve into the emotional aftermath of divorce and explore the transformative power of self-care in promoting healing, self-discovery, and personal growth during this challenging life transition.

## The Emotional Aftermath of Divorce

Divorce marks the end of a significant chapter in one's life, often accompanied by a range of intense emotions such as grief, anger, sadness, and confusion. Coping with the emotional aftermath of a divorce can be an arduous journey. Still, it is also an opportunity for individuals to prioritize their well-being and embark on self-discovery and empowerment.

## Grieving the Loss

The end of a marriage can feel like losing a close relationship, dreams, and a shared future. It's essential to allow oneself to grieve this loss. Grieving is a natural process that can help individuals accept their new reality. This process may involve experiencing a variety of emotions, from denial and anger to bargaining, depression, and eventually acceptance. Each person's grieving process is unique, and it's important to honor your own pace and feelings.

## Emotional Rollercoaster

Divorce often brings a whirlwind of emotions that can feel overwhelming. Anger, sadness, confusion, relief, and fear may all surface at different times. It's crucial to recognize that these emotions are normal and a part of the healing process. Acknowledging and understanding these emotions can help individuals navigate through them more effectively.

## The Role of Self-Care

Self-care practices play a crucial role in supporting individuals during this challenging time. By engaging in intentional self-care, individuals can nurture their emotional well-being and foster healing from the effects of divorce. Self-care is not just about pampering oneself but involves taking proactive steps to maintain and improve overall health and well-being.

## Acknowledging and Honoring Emotions

A critical aspect of self-care after divorce involves acknowledging and honoring one's emotions. Creating a safe space to process and express feelings is essential, whether through journaling, therapy or talking with trusted friends and family members. Allowing yourself to grieve and heal is vital to rebuilding and finding emotional balance.

**Journaling**

Journaling is a powerful tool for processing emotions. Writing down thoughts and feelings can provide clarity and a sense of relief. It allows individuals to express themselves freely without judgment. Regular journaling can also track progress and reflect on the journey of healing.

**Therapy and Counseling**

Seeking professional help through therapy or counseling can provide a safe and supportive environment to explore and process emotions. Therapists can offer valuable insights, coping strategies, and support throughout the healing process. Therapy can help address more profound issues, such as unresolved conflicts or patterns that may have contributed to the divorce.

**Talking with Trusted Friends and Family**

Talking with trusted friends and family members can provide emotional support and validation. Sharing your experiences and feelings with those who care about you can help alleviate isolation and provide comfort.

**Physical Self-Care**

Self-care also encompasses taking care of your physical well-being. Prioritizing healthy habits such as regular exercise, nutritious eating, and sufficient rest can provide a foundation of stability and support during this time of transition. Physical self-care not only has the potential to improve your overall well-being but also boosts your self-esteem and resilience as you navigate the challenges of divorce.

- **Regular Exercise-**Exercise is a powerful tool for managing stress and improving mood. Physical activity releases endorphins, which are natural mood lifters. Regular exercise can enhance sleep quality, increase energy levels, and boost self-esteem. Finding an exercise routine you enjoy, whether walking, jogging, yoga, or dancing, can make it easier to stick with.
- **Nutritious Eating-**Eating a balanced and nutritious diet is essential for overall health and well-being. Proper nutrition can help manage stress, improve energy levels, and support mental health. Focusing on whole foods, such as fruits, vegetables, lean proteins, and whole grains, can provide the nutrients needed for optimal health.

- **Sufficient Rest-** rest and sleep are crucial for physical and emotional recovery. Sleep is also essential for cognitive function, mood regulation, and overall health. Creating a restful sleep environment and establishing a regular sleep routine can improve sleep quality.

## Self-Discovery and Personal Growth

Self-care practices that promote self-discovery and personal growth are invaluable during this period. Engaging in activities that inspire you, such as pursuing hobbies, learning new skills, or exploring creative outlets, can help you reconnect with your interests and passions and rediscover your sense of self.

## Pursuing Hobbies

Rediscovering or exploring new hobbies can provide joy and a sense of accomplishment. Engaging in activities you enjoy can be a powerful form of self-care, providing a break from stress and an opportunity to focus on something positive.

- **Learning New Skills-** Learning new skills can boost self-confidence and provide a sense of purpose. Whether taking a class, learning a new language, or picking up a musical instrument, challenging yourself to learn something new can be rewarding and enriching.
- **Creative Outlets-** Creative activities, such as painting, writing, music, or crafting, can be therapeutic. Creative expression allows for releasing emotions and can be a powerful way to process feelings and experiences.

## Establishing Healthy Boundaries

Boundaries are essential in self-care during and after divorce. Establishing healthy boundaries helps maintain emotional well-being and prevents further stress and turmoil. It may involve setting clear limits with your ex-partner, managing communication channels, and protecting your space and time for self-care.

- **Setting Limits with Your Ex-Partner-** Setting boundaries with your ex-partner is crucial for emotional recovery. It might involve limiting communication to necessary topics, such as co-parenting, and establishing clear interaction guidelines. It's important to communicate these boundaries clearly and stick to them to protect your emotional well-being.

- **Managing Communication Channels-** Communication channels like phone, email, or social media can help reduce stress and maintain boundaries. Choosing the most appropriate and least stressful method of communication can help prevent misunderstandings and conflicts.
- **Protecting Your Space and Time**—Creating and protecting your personal space and time for self-care is essential. It might involve setting aside daily time for relaxation, hobbies, or self-reflection. Ensuring that you have a physical space where you feel comfortable and safe can also support your emotional well-being.

**Building a Support Network**

Building a support network is a vital aspect of self-care during divorce. Surrounding yourself with trusted friends, family, or support groups can offer a sense of community, validation, and empathy. Sharing your experiences with others who have gone through similar **situations can provide comfort and guidance throughout your journey.**

- **Trusted Friends and Family-** Trusted friends and family can provide emotional support, practical help, and a sense of belonging. Open communication and mutual support can strengthen these relationships and provide a strong foundation during the transition.
- **Support Groups-** Joining support groups for individuals going through divorce can provide a sense of community and shared experience. These groups can offer practical advice, emotional support, and encouragement from others who understand the challenges of divorce.
- **Professional Support**—**In addition to** friends and family, seeking support from professionals, such as therapists, counselors, or life coaches, can provide valuable insights and guidance. Professional support can help address specific challenges and provide tailored strategies for coping and healing.

**Empowering Oneself through Knowledge**

Empowering oneself through knowledge is another crucial aspect of self-care during divorce. Educating oneself about the legal process, financial planning, and coping mechanisms can help individuals make informed decisions and actively participate in their journey.

- **Understanding the Legal Process-** Understanding the legal process of divorce can reduce anxiety and help individuals feel more in control. Educating oneself about the steps involved, legal rights, and

options can provide clarity and empower individuals to make informed decisions.
- ➢ **Financial Planning**—Divorce often brings significant financial changes. Developing a financial plan can help manage these changes and provide stability. It might involve creating a budget, understanding financial obligations, and planning for future financial goals.
- ➢ **Learning Coping Mechanisms**—Learning about coping mechanisms for managing stress, emotions, and challenges can enhance resilience and well-being. These might include stress management techniques, relaxation exercises, and lifestyle modifications.

## Moving Forward with Self-Care

Through self-care practices, individuals can transform the aftermath of divorce into an opportunity for personal growth and empowerment. By nurturing your emotional well-being, exploring new interests, setting healthy boundaries, and finding a supportive network, you take decisive steps towards rebuilding your life and embracing a future filled with possibilities.

## Integrating Self-Care into Daily Life

Integrating self-care into daily routines can ensure these practices become a consistent part of life. It might involve setting aside time daily for self-care activities, creating a supportive environment, and regularly reassessing self-care needs and strategies.

## Creating a Self-Care Plan

Creating a self-care plan can help individuals prioritize and structure their self-care activities. A self-care plan might include various practices, such as scheduling regular exercise, setting aside time for hobbies, and planning regular check-ins with a therapist. By having a plan, individuals can ensure they are consistently engaging in activities that support their mental health.

## Adapting to Life Changes

Life changes and unexpected challenges can impact self-care routines. Adaptability and willingness to adjust self-care practices in response to life changes are essential. It might involve seeking additional support during stressful periods or modifying routines to accommodate new responsibilities.

## Continuing the Journey

The following chapters will explore self-care practices tailored to different life experiences, including mental health challenges, cancer, and more. These chapters offer guidance and support in embracing self-care during times of difficulty and transition. Individuals can build a strong foundation for overall well-being and resilience by continuing to prioritize self-care.

**Commitment to Self-Care**

A commitment to self-care is a commitment to one's health and well-being. It is an ongoing journey that requires dedication and self-compassion. By making self-care a priority, individuals can enhance their lives.

# Chapter 6: Setting Boundaries for Self-Care

This chapter will explore the importance of establishing and maintaining healthy boundaries as part of self-care. Boundaries act as protective barriers safeguarding our well-being, ensuring our physical, emotional, and mental needs are met.

**Understanding the Role of Boundaries**

Understanding the role of boundaries is fundamental in promoting self-care. Boundaries serve as a framework for navigating relationships, personal space, and emotional safety. By defining and communicating our limits effectively, we create a healthy balance between giving and receiving, fostering mutually respectful connections with others.

- **Personal Relationships-** Establishing boundaries is crucial in various aspects of life. For instance, in personal relationships, setting boundaries helps maintain healthy dynamics and safeguards against emotional harm. It involves recognizing and communicating what is acceptable and unacceptable, allowing us to maintain a sense of autonomy and self-respect. Healthy boundaries in relationships ensure that both parties feel valued and respected, preventing codependency and fostering mutual growth.
- **Professional Life-** Boundaries also extend to our professional lives. Establishing limitations at work helps protect our time and energy, prevent burnout, and ensure a healthy work-life balance. It involves setting realistic expectations, asserting when necessary, and creating space for self-care routines outside of work. Effective professional boundaries might include setting precise work hours, delegating tasks, and learning to say no to additional responsibilities that compromise personal well-being.
- **Physical and Emotional Health-** Boundaries help us prioritize our well-being and prevent overextending ourselves in self-care. By setting limits on our commitments and recognizing our physical and emotional limitations, we can ensure we have the resources and energy to engage in self-care practices that nourish us. It might involve limiting social engagements when feeling overwhelmed, saying no to activities that cause stress, or creating a quiet time for relaxation and rejuvenation.
- **Establishing and Communicating Boundaries-** Maintaining healthy boundaries involves regular self-reflection and communication. We

must check in with ourselves, assess how our limits are respected, and adjust as needed. When our boundaries are consistently violated, it is crucial to communicate our needs and reinforce boundaries assertively, even if it feels uncomfortable or challenging.

### Self-Reflection

Regular self-reflection is essential for recognizing when boundaries must be set or adjusted. This process involves evaluating personal needs, identifying stressors, and understanding emotional triggers. Keeping a journal or practicing mindfulness can help increase self-awareness and provide insights into necessary boundary adjustments.

### Communication

Effective communication is critical to setting and maintaining boundaries. Clearly and assertively expressing your needs and limits to others can prevent misunderstandings and ensure your boundaries are respected. Using "I" statements, such as "I need some time to myself" or "I am not comfortable with this," can help convey your message without sounding confrontational.

### Enforcing Boundaries

Enforcing boundaries may require reiteration and consistency. When others overstep your boundaries, calmly remind them of your limits and the importance of respecting them. It might involve setting consequences for repeated violations or seeking support from others to reinforce your boundaries.

### Boundaries in Different Contexts

Boundaries can vary depending on the context, and it's essential to understand how to set and maintain them in different areas of life.

- **Family Boundaries**—Family relationships can be complex, and setting boundaries with family members can be challenging but necessary. This might involve limiting the frequency of visits, establishing rules for communication, or deciding what topics are off-limits for discussion.
- **Social Boundaries**—Social boundaries help manage interactions with friends and acquaintances. They can include setting limits on social media use, deciding how much personal information to share, and choosing how to spend your social time.

- **Digital Boundaries**—In the digital age, setting boundaries online is crucial. This includes managing screen time, controlling who has access to your personal information, and deciding which digital interactions are healthy and beneficial.

**The Benefits of Healthy Boundaries**

Setting and maintaining healthy boundaries have numerous benefits for well-being and personal growth.

- **Improved Relationships**- Healthy boundaries contribute to more respectful and fulfilling relationships. When boundaries are clear, relationships can thrive on mutual understanding and respect, reducing conflicts and misunderstandings.
- **Enhanced Self-Esteem**- Establishing boundaries helps build self-respect and self-worth. By valuing your own needs and limits, you reinforce a positive self-image and increase confidence in your ability to manage your life.
- **Reduced Stress**—Boundaries help manage stress by preventing overcommitment and ensuring time and energy for self-care. By protecting your personal space and time, you can maintain a healthier and more balanced lifestyle.
- **Greater Autonomy**- Boundaries empower you to take control of your life and make decisions that align with your values and needs. This autonomy fosters personal growth and allows you to live authentically.
- **Challenges in Setting Boundaries**- While setting boundaries is crucial, it can also be challenging, especially for those who have not practiced it before.
- **Fear of Conflict**- Many avoid setting boundaries out of fear of conflict or rejection. It's important to remember that healthy relationships involve honest communication, and setting boundaries can ultimately strengthen connections.

**Guilt**

Some individuals may feel guilty about setting boundaries, believing they are selfish. However, self-care and setting boundaries are essential for maintaining personal well-being and effectively supporting others. Setting boundaries can initially feel awkward or uncomfortable for those unfamiliar. Practice and patience are crucial to becoming more confident in establishing and maintaining boundaries.

**Practical Tips for Setting Boundaries**

To successfully establish and maintain boundaries, consider the following practical tips:

- ➤ **Start Small-** Begin by setting small, manageable boundaries and gradually work up to more significant ones. It can help build confidence and make the process feel less overwhelming.
- ➤ **Be Consistent-** Consistency is crucial in maintaining boundaries. Ensure you consistently enforce your limits and do not make exceptions that compromise your well-being.
- ➤ **Seek Support—**Enlist the help of friends, family, or a therapist to help you set and maintain boundaries. A support system can provide encouragement and accountability.
- ➤ **Practice Self-Compassion-** Be kind to yourself as you set boundaries. Understand that it's a learning experience, and making adjustments along the way is okay.

**Moving Forward with Boundaries**

In the following chapters, we will further explore self-care practices that complement the establishment of healthy boundaries. Integrating these practices into our lives allows us to cultivate a strong sense of self, protect our well-being, and foster meaningful relationships and personal growth.

**Continuing the Journey**

Setting boundaries is an ongoing process that requires regular reassessment and adjustment. As life circumstances change, so too may your boundaries. By staying attuned to your needs and consistently practicing self-care, you can ensure that your boundaries support your well-being.

**Embracing Change**

Embracing change and being flexible with your boundaries can help you adapt to new situations and maintain balance. Remember that boundaries are not rigid rules but guidelines that can evolve with your needs.

**Commitment to Self-Care**

A commitment to self-care includes setting and maintaining healthy boundaries. You create a foundation for a healthier, more fulfilling life by prioritizing your well-being and respecting your limits.

# Chapter 7: Building a Supportive Network in Self-Care

This chapter will explore the significance of social support in times of adversity, and the strategies to cultivate meaningful relationships and seek help during challenging life transitions as a crucial aspect of self-care.

## The Importance of Social Support

Human beings are fundamentally social creatures, and having a supportive network of relationships can significantly impact our well-being, especially during difficult times. Cultivating a solid support system is essential for promoting self-care and resilience. Recognizing the significance of social support is the first step in fostering a network of relationships that provide comfort, guidance, and understanding. Emotional support can help reduce feelings of loneliness, anxiety, and depression. Knowing that others care about you and are there to support you can provide a sense of security and belonging.

## Practical Benefits

Social support also offers practical benefits. Friends, family, and community members can provide assistance with daily tasks, offer advice, and share resources. This helps reduce stress and allow individuals to focus more on self-care and healing processes.

## Enhancing Resilience

A supportive network can enhance resilience by providing a buffer against stress and adversity. Supportive relationships offer encouragement, validation, and perspective, helping individuals navigate challenges more effectively.

## Strategies for Building a Supportive Network

Building a supportive network involves several strategies. The first is identifying individuals who can provide emotional support and understanding. It may include close friends, family members, or support groups tailored to your challenges. Reach out to those who have demonstrated empathy and willingness to listen without judgment.

## Identifying Supportive Individuals

Recognize the people in your life who have been supportive and understanding in the past. These individuals are likely to be empathetic and reliable sources of support during challenging times. It is essential to choose those who respect your boundaries and provide a nonjudgmental space to express yourself.

## Effective Communication

Effective communication plays a vital role in building and maintaining supportive relationships. Clearly expressing your needs, emotions, and boundaries can facilitate understanding and help others provide the support you require. Be open and honest about your struggles and allow yourself to be vulnerable when reaching out for help.

- **Expressing Needs-** Communicating your needs effectively involves being clear and specific. Let others know what kind of support you seek, whether emotional, practical, or informational. For example, you might say, "I need someone to talk to about my feelings," or "I could use some help with household chores."
- **Active Listening-** Active listening is equally important in building supportive relationships. Practice empathetic listening, wherein you engage fully with others' experiences, validate their emotions, and provide a safe space for them to express themselves. Show genuine interest and ask follow-up questions to foster deep connections.
- **Engaging in Reciprocity in Relationships-** Engaging in reciprocity is another strategy to cultivate a supportive network. Remember that support is a two-way street, and being there for others in need creates a foundation of trust and mutual understanding. Offer help, encouragement, and practical assistance to those in your network. Supporting others fosters a sense of connection and strengthens the bonds within your network. Reciprocity can take many forms, including:
- **Emotional Support**—Providing emotional support can be as simple as listening to a friend's concerns, offering a shoulder to cry on, or validating their feelings. Being present and empathetic helps create a safe space for others to express themselves and feel understood.

Offering practical assistance, such as helping with chores, providing transportation, or sharing resources, can significantly impact someone's life. This tangible support demonstrates care and reliability, reinforcing the strength of your relationship. Encouraging others, celebrating their successes, and motivating them through challenging times can boost their morale and resilience. Positive reinforcement and genuine appreciation contribute to a supportive and uplifting environment.

In addition to personal relationships, consider seeking professional support when necessary. Therapists, counselors, and support groups can provide specialized guidance and expertise during difficult life transitions. These professionals can help you navigate your challenges and provide tailored strategies for self-care. Therapists and counselors offer a safe, confidential space to explore your feelings, identify coping strategies, and develop a plan for moving forward. They can help address specific issues, such as anxiety, depression, or trauma, and provide tools to enhance your mental well-being. Joining support groups allows you to connect with others experiencing similar challenges. These groups offer community, shared experiences, and practical advice. Support groups can be found for various issues, including grief, addiction, mental health, and chronic illness.

Lastly, technology offers an array of opportunities for building a supportive network. Online communities, forums, and social media groups centered around shared experiences can connect individuals facing similar challenges. Engaging in these virtual communities can provide a sense of belonging, camaraderie, and support, even from a distance. Online communities and forums provide a platform for individuals to share their stories, seek advice, and offer support. These communities can be precious for those who may not have access to local support groups or who prefer the anonymity of online interactions. Social media groups focused on specific topics or experiences can help you connect with like-minded individuals. These groups often provide resources, inspiration, and a sense of community. Participating in discussions and sharing your journey can foster connections and provide emotional support. Virtual support groups, conducted through video conferencing platforms, offer the benefits of traditional support groups with the convenience of remote access. These groups can provide structured support guided by a facilitator, allowing for real-time interaction and connection.

## The Benefits of a Supportive Network

Building a supportive network has numerous benefits for overall well-being and personal growth.

## Enhanced Emotional Well-Being

A strong support network can significantly enhance one's emotional well-being. Knowing that one has people who care about one and are available to provide support can alleviate feelings of loneliness, reduce stress, and improve one's mood. A supportive network can increase resilience by giving encouragement, perspective, and practical help during difficult times.

This support can help you cope more effectively with challenges and bounce back quickly from setbacks.

**Sense of Belonging**

A supportive network fosters a sense of belonging and connection, essential for mental and emotional health. Feeling part of a community can provide a sense of purpose and contribute to overall happiness. Engaging with a supportive network can promote personal growth by exposing you to new ideas, perspectives, and experiences. These interactions can inspire self-reflection, learning, and development. While building a supportive network is crucial, it can also be challenging, especially for those who are naturally introverted or have had negative relationship experiences.

**Overcoming Social Anxiety**

Social anxiety can make it difficult to reach out and build new connections. To gradually build confidence in social interactions, taking small steps, such as attending social events with a trusted friend or joining a low-pressure online community is essential.

**Dealing with Rejection**

Fear of rejection can hinder efforts to build a support network. Remember that not everyone will be a perfect match, and it's okay to seek out different connections until you find those who are genuinely supportive and understanding.

**Balancing Support with Independence**

It's essential to strike a balance between seeking support and maintaining independence. While a supportive network is valuable, developing self-reliance and confidence in managing your challenges is also crucial.

**Practical Tips for Building a Supportive Network**

To successfully build and maintain a supportive network, consider the following practical tips:

- ➤ **Be Genuine-**Authenticity is critical to building meaningful connections. Be yourself and share your true thoughts and feelings with others. Genuine relationships are built on trust and honesty.
- ➤ **Reach Out Regularly-** Maintaining relationships requires regular communication. Make an effort to reach out to your support network

regularly through phone calls, messages, or in-person meetings. Consistent interaction helps strengthen bonds and shows that you care.
- **Show Appreciation-** Express gratitude to those who support you. A simple thank you, or a thoughtful gesture can go a long way in maintaining positive relationships. Acknowledging others' efforts reinforces the value of your connection.
- **Be Patient**- Building a supportive network takes time. Be patient and persistent in your efforts to cultivate relationships. Finding the right people who align with your values and needs may take time.
- **Leverage Existing Relationships**- Be more open and communicative to strengthen and expand your current relationships. Deepening existing connections can sometimes provide the support you need without seeking new relationships.

By actively building a supportive network, you create a community of individuals dedicated to your well-being, growth, and self-care. These connections provide emotional support, guidance, and validation, enhancing your resilience and ability to navigate challenging life transitions with strength and grace. Integrating support into your daily life involves making time for regular interactions with your support network, seeking help when needed, and offering support in return. This ongoing engagement ensures that your network remains firm and supportive.

As life circumstances change, so too may your support needs. Be open to adjusting your network and seeking new connections as necessary. Flexibility and adaptability are vital to maintaining a robust support system. A commitment to self-care includes building and maintaining a supportive network. Prioritizing these relationships creates a foundation for a healthier, more fulfilling life. By actively building a supportive network, you make a community of individuals dedicated to your well-being, growth, and self-care. These connections provide emotional support, guidance, and validation, enhancing your resilience and ability to navigate challenging life transitions with strength and grace.

In the following chapters, we will explore self-care practices that complement the support of a network. By integrating these practices into your life and cultivating meaningful relationships, you can foster a robust support system that nurtures your well-being and empowers you to navigate life's challenges more easily.

# Chapter 8: Cultivating Mindfulness in Self-Care

This chapter will explore mindfulness's profound benefits in promoting self-awareness and resilience and how integrating mindfulness techniques into daily self-care routines can enhance overall well-being.

**Understanding Mindfulness**

Mindfulness is being fully present at the moment, nonjudgmentally, and with a gentle curiosity. It involves compassionate and accepting attention to thoughts, emotions, and sensations. Mindfulness is not about emptying the mind or achieving a calm state but rather about noticing whatever arises with openness and curiosity. Numerous studies have demonstrated mindfulness's benefits for mental and physical health. Mindfulness can reduce symptoms of anxiety and depression, lower blood pressure, improve sleep, and enhance overall well-being. It works by helping individuals become more aware of their thoughts and feelings, allowing them to respond to stressors more effectively rather than reacting impulsively.

**The Role of Mindfulness in Self-Care**

Mindfulness practice can significantly enhance self-care by promoting self-awareness and helping us stay attuned to our physical, emotional, and mental needs. Through mindfulness, we develop a deep understanding of ourselves, our triggers, and our patterns of thinking and behaving.

> **Promoting Self-Awareness**
> One of the primary benefits of mindfulness is increased self-awareness. By regularly tuning into our thoughts and feelings, we can better understand our needs and make more informed choices about our self-care. Heightened awareness helps us recognize when we feel stressed, overwhelmed, or need a break.

> **Enhancing Emotional Regulation**
> Mindfulness helps us to have greater emotional regulation. By observing our emotions without judgment, we can learn to respond to them in healthier ways. It can reduce the intensity and duration of negative emotions and enhance our ability to experience positive emotions.

> **Building Resilience**
> One critical advantage of mindfulness practice is its ability to promote resilience. By cultivating the ability to be fully present

and accepting of our experiences, we strengthen our capacity to navigate challenging situations with more clarity and composure. Mindfulness helps us regulate our emotions, reduce stress, and improve our ability to cope with life's ups and downs.

**Practical Mindfulness Techniques**

Integrating mindfulness techniques into daily self-care routines can transform our well-being. Here are some practical ways to incorporate mindfulness into your self-care practices:

- **Mindful Breathing:** Focus on your breath briefly each day. Notice the sensation of the breath entering and leaving your body. Allow yourself to observe your breath without judgment or needing to change it. This simple practice can help ground you in the present moment and bring a sense of calm.
- **Technique: The 4-7-8 Breath-** The 4-7-8 breath is a simple yet powerful technique for calming the mind and body. Inhale quietly through the nose for a count of 4, hold the breath for a count of 7, and exhale completely through the mouth for a count of 8. Repeat this cycle three to four times.
- **Body Scan Meditation-** Set aside time to tune into your body. Start from the top of your head and gradually move your attention down, noticing any sensations or areas of tension or relaxation. Pay attention to each part of your body and observe without judgment. This practice promotes self-awareness and relaxation.

**Technique: Guided Body Scan**

Many guided body scan meditations are available online and through meditation apps. These can help you systematically focus on different body parts, promoting deep relaxation and awareness.

**Mindful Eating**

Slow down and fully engage your senses while eating. Notice the flavors, textures, and smells of your food. Pay attention to the physical sensations of chewing and swallowing. Eating mindfully can help you reconnect with your body's cues of hunger and fullness while savoring the experience of nourishing yourself.

### Technique: The Raisin Exercise

A classic mindfulness exercise involves eating a raisin slowly and mindfully. Please pay attention to its texture, smell, and taste, and notice the sensations as you chew and swallow. This exercise can be applied to any meal to cultivate mindful eating habits.

### Mindful Movement

Engage in activities such as yoga, walking, or tai chi, focusing on the sensations in your body as you move. Notice the rhythmic flow of your breath and the way your body responds to the movement. This practice helps cultivate a mind-body connection and promotes grounding and relaxation.

### Technique: Walking Meditation

Walking meditation involves walking slowly and deliberately, paying attention to each step and the sensations in your body. You can practice this in your home, yard, or park, allowing yourself to be fully present with each step.

### Mindful Journaling

Take time to write down your thoughts and emotions without judgment or the need to edit. Allow yourself to express yourself freely, using writing as a tool for self-reflection and self-expression. This practice can help you gain insights and process emotions effectively.

### Technique: Stream of Consciousness Writing

Set a timer for 10-15 minutes and write continuously without worrying about grammar or punctuation. Let your thoughts flow onto the page without censorship. It can help release pent-up emotions and clarify your thoughts.

### Integrating Mindfulness into Daily Life

Mindfulness is a skill that requires consistent practice and patience. Here are some tips for integrating mindfulness into your daily routine:

- **Start Small-** Begin with short mindfulness practices, such as a few minutes of mindful breathing or a quick body scan. Gradually increase the duration and frequency of your mindfulness sessions as you become more comfortable with the practice.
- **Create a Routine-** Incorporate mindfulness into your daily routine by setting aside specific times for practice, such as first thing in the morning or before bed. Consistency helps establish mindfulness as a regular part of your self-care regimen.

- **Be Patient and Compassionate-** Remember that cultivating mindfulness is a journey that requires patience and self-compassion. It's normal for the mind to wander during mindfulness practice. When this happens, gently bring your focus back to the present moment without self-judgment.
- **Use Reminders-** Place reminders in your environment, such as sticky notes or phone alerts, to prompt you to practice mindfulness throughout the day. These reminders can help you stay mindful even during busy times.

## Incorporate Mindfulness into Everyday Activities

Practice mindfulness during everyday activities, such as brushing teeth, washing dishes, or commuting. Pay attention to the sensations, sounds, and smells associated with these tasks, bringing your full awareness to the present moment.

## The Long-Term Benefits of Mindfulness

Incorporating mindfulness into your self-care routine can profoundly affect your overall well-being. It can allow you to become more attuned to your needs, boost your resilience, and live a more fulfilling and present-centered life.

- **Enhanced Emotional Well-Being-** Mindfulness practice can lead to a greater sense of emotional balance and well-being. By becoming more aware of your emotions and learning to respond to them with compassion, you can reduce the impact of stress and negative emotions on your life.
- **Improved Physical Health** Mindfulness has been shown to have numerous physical health benefits, including reduced blood pressure, improved sleep, and enhanced immune function. Regular mindfulness practice can contribute to better overall health and vitality.
- **Stronger Relationships** Mindfulness can enhance your relationships by improving your ability to listen, communicate, and empathize. Being fully present with loved ones fosters deeper connections and more meaningful interactions.
- **Greater Self-Awareness and Personal Growth-** Mindfulness promotes self-awareness and personal growth by helping you understand your thoughts, behaviors, and motivations. This self-knowledge can lead to positive changes in your life and greater alignment with your values and goals.

**Long-Term Resilience**

Cultivating mindfulness strengthens one's ability to cope with life's challenges. Staying present and accepting one's experiences builds resilience and develops a more balanced and grounded approach to adversity.

**Moving Forward with Mindfulness**

In the following chapters, we will explore self-care practices tailored to nurturing physical well-being and emotional balance and finding meaning and purpose in life. These chapters provide comprehensive guidance to help you flourish in your self-care journey.

**Continuing the Practice**

Commit to incorporating mindfulness into your daily life and continue to explore different mindfulness techniques. Regular practice will deepen your mindfulness skills and enhance your overall well-being. Consider sharing mindfulness practices with friends and family. Practicing mindfulness together can strengthen relationships and create a supportive community. Remember that mindfulness is a lifelong journey. Embrace each step of the process, knowing that every moment of mindfulness contributes to a healthier, happier, and more fulfilling life.

# Chapter 9: Prioritizing Physical Self-Care

In this chapter, we will explore the significant impact of physical well-being on overall mental and emotional health and the importance of incorporating physical self-care practices into our daily lives to promote restoration and vitality.

The mind and body are deeply interconnected. Taking care of our physical well-being is a crucial aspect of self-care, as it directly influences our mental and emotional health. When we prioritize physical self-care, we create a solid foundation for overall well-being, enabling us to navigate life's challenges with resilience and vigor. Research has shown that physical health significantly affects mental health. Regular physical activity, proper nutrition, adequate sleep, and hydration can improve mood, reduce anxiety and depression, and enhance cognitive function. Conversely, neglecting physical health can lead to increased stress, fatigue, and mental health issues.

**Physical Self-Care Practices**

Physical self-care practices encompass a wide range of activities that promote restoration and vitality. These practices may include:

**Exercise-** Regular physical activity improves physical fitness and profoundly affects mental well-being. Exercise releases endorphins, the body's natural "feel-good" chemicals, which can boost mood, reduce stress, and improve cognitive function. Find activities you enjoy, whether walking, dancing, yoga, or team sports, and make them a regular part of your self-care routine.

**Types of Exercise-**
- **Aerobic Exercise:** Running, swimming, and cycling increase your heart rate and improve cardiovascular health. These exercises help reduce stress and anxiety and improve overall mood.
- **Strength Training:** Weightlifting, resistance band, and bodyweight exercises build muscle strength and endurance. Strength training can boost self-esteem and promote a sense of accomplishment.
- **Flexibility Exercises**: Yoga, Pilates, and stretching exercises enhance flexibility, reduce muscle tension, and improve overall physical function. These exercises also promote relaxation and mindfulness.

### Creating a Routine

Incorporate different types of exercise into your routine to address various aspects of physical fitness. Aim for at least 150 minutes of moderate aerobic activity or 75 minutes of vigorous activity each week, along with strength training exercises twice a week. Remember to start slowly and gradually increasing your workouts' intensity and duration.

Prioritizing sufficient and restful sleep is crucial for physical and mental rejuvenation. Establish healthy sleep habits, such as sticking to a consistent sleep schedule, creating a relaxing bedtime routine, and ensuring a comfortable sleep environment. Adequate sleep enhances cognitive function, emotional balance, and overall well-being.

### Sleep Hygiene Tips

- **Consistent Schedule**: Go to bed and wake up simultaneously every day, even on weekends. It helps regulate your body's internal clock and improves sleep quality.
- **Bedtime Routine**: Develop a relaxing routine before bed to signal your body that it's time to wind down. Its might include reading, warm bathing, or practicing gentle yoga.
- **Sleep Environment**: Ensure your bedroom is dark, quiet, and relaxed. Invest in a comfortable mattress and pillows to create an optimal sleep environment.
- **Limiting Stimulants:** Avoid caffeine, nicotine, and heavy meals close to bedtime. These can interfere with your ability to fall and stay asleep.

### Nutrition

Nourishing your body with a balanced and nutritious diet is essential to physical self-care. Focus on incorporating fruits, vegetables, whole grains, lean proteins, and healthy fats into your meals. Pay attention to your body's hunger and fullness cues, and practice mindful eating to foster a healthy relationship with food.

### Healthy Eating Habits

- **Balanced Meals:** Aim to include a variety of food groups in each meal to ensure you are getting a range of nutrients. A balanced plate might consist of a serving of lean protein, a portion of whole grains, and plenty of fruits and vegetables.

- ➤ **Portion Control:** Pay attention to portion sizes to avoid overeating. Using smaller plates and bowls can help regulate portion sizes naturally.
- ➤ **Mindful Eating:** Slow down and savor your meals. Pay attention to the flavors, textures, and aromas of your food. Eating mindfully can help you enjoy your meals more and recognize when you are full.
- ➤ **Hydration**: Drink plenty of water throughout the day to stay hydrated. Aim for at least eight 8-ounce glasses of water daily, and more if you are active or live in a hot climate.

## Hydration

Staying hydrated is often overlooked but is crucial in maintaining physical health. Drink adequate water throughout the day to support proper bodily functions, improve concentration, and promote overall well-being.

## Benefits of Hydration

- ➤ **Cognitive Function:** Proper hydration is essential for maintaining concentration, memory, and overall cognitive function.
- ➤ **Physical Performance:** Staying hydrated helps regulate body temperature, lubricate joints, and prevent muscle cramps, improving physical performance.
- ➤ **Mood and Energy Levels:** Dehydration can lead to fatigue and irritability. Drinking enough water helps maintain energy levels and a positive mood.
- ➤ **Skin Health**: Adequate hydration supports healthy skin by keeping it moisturized and promoting a youthful appearance.

## Body Awareness

Cultivating a mindful awareness of your body is another aspect of physical self-care. Take moments throughout the day to check in with your body, noticing any areas of tension or discomfort. Practice relaxation techniques such as deep breathing, stretching, or self-massage to release stress and promote physical well-being.

## Techniques for Body Awareness

Deep Breathing: To reduce stress and promote relaxation, practice deep breathing exercises. Inhale deeply through your nose, hold your breath for a few seconds, and exhale slowly through your mouth.

- ➤ **Stretching**: Incorporate stretching into your daily routine to release muscle tension and improve flexibility. Focus on stretching all major

muscle groups, especially those that tend to become tight from prolonged sitting or repetitive movements.
- ➤ **Self-Massage:** Use techniques like foam rolling or gentle massage to relieve muscle tension and promote relaxation. Pay attention to areas that feel particularly tight or sore.

**Screen Time Management**

In today's digital age, it is important to practice moderation and set boundaries with screen time. Excessive screen time can negatively impact sleep patterns, strain eyes, and contribute to sedentary behavior. Allocate time for engaging in activities that do not involve screens, such as reading, outdoor walks, or hobbies, to promote physical movement and reduce screen-related stress.

**Tips for Managing Screen Time**

- ➤ **Set Limits**: Establish specific times of the day when you will use screens and stick to these limits. Use screen time tracking apps to monitor and manage your usage.
- ➤ **Take Breaks:** Follow the 20-20-20 rule: every 20 minutes, take a 20-second break to look at something 20 feet away. It helps reduce eye strain and mental fatigue.
- ➤ **Create Screen-Free Zones**: Designate specific areas of your home, such as the bedroom or dining area, as screen-free zones to promote relaxation and social interaction.
- ➤ **Engage in Offline Activities:** Make time for activities that do not involve screens, such as exercising, cooking, gardening, or spending time with loved ones.

**Integrating Physical Self-Care into Daily Life**

By prioritizing physical self-care, we improve our physical health and create a solid mental and emotional well-being foundation. These practices promote restoration, vitality, and resilience in navigating life's challenges.

**Creating a Personalized Self-Care Plan**

Developing a personalized self-care plan can help you integrate physical self-care practices into your daily life. Consider the following steps:

- ➤ **Assess Your Needs**: Reflect on your current physical health and identify areas that need attention. It might include improving your diet, increasing physical activity, or establishing better sleep habits.

- **Set Goals**: Establish specific, achievable goals for your physical self-care. These goals should be realistic and tailored to your individual needs and preferences.
- **Develop a Routine:** Create a daily or weekly routine incorporating self-care practices. Consistency is critical to making self-care a regular part of your life.
- **Monitor Progress**: Track your progress and adjust as needed. Regularly evaluate how your self-care practices are impacting your overall well-being.

## Overcoming Barriers to Physical Self-Care

Implementing physical self-care practices can sometimes be challenging. Here are some common barriers and strategies to overcome them:

- **Lack of Time**: Prioritize self-care by scheduling it into your day, just like any other important activity. Even short bursts of activity, such as a 10-minute walk, can be beneficial.
- **Motivation:** Find activities you enjoy and set achievable goals to stay motivated. Consider enlisting a friend or family member to join you for added support and accountability.
- **Physical Limitations:** Adapt self-care practices to accommodate any physical limitations. Consult with a healthcare provider or fitness professional for personalized advice.
- **Stress and Fatigue:** Recognize that stress and fatigue can make self-care more challenging. Focus on activities that help manage stress and boost energy levels, such as gentle exercise, relaxation techniques, and adequate sleep.

## The Long-Term Benefits of Physical Self-Care

Prioritizing physical self-care offers numerous long-term benefits for overall health and well-being:

- **Enhanced Mental Health**: Regular physical activity and proper nutrition support mental health by reducing symptoms of anxiety and depression, improving mood, and enhancing cognitive function.
- **Increased Resilience**: A strong foundation of physical health enhances your ability to cope with stress and adversity, promoting greater resilience and emotional stability.
- **Improved Quality of Life:** Physical self-care practices contribute to a higher quality of life by improving physical health, boosting energy levels, and promoting well-being.

- Greater Longevity: Regular physical activity, a nutritious diet, and adequate sleep can contribute to a longer, healthier life.

**Moving Forward with Physical Self-Care**

In the following chapters, we will further explore self-care practices tailored to emotional well-being, finding meaning and purpose, and sustaining self-care for long-term well-being. These chapters provide comprehensive guidance to support you in your self-care journey.

# Chapter 10: Nurturing Emotional Self-Care

This chapter will explore the necessity of nurturing emotional well-being during adversity and the importance of crafting inspirational self-care rituals. These rituals aim to foster emotional growth, self-compassion, and resilience.

## The Importance of Emotional Well-Being

Emotional well-being is at the core of self-care, especially during challenging times. When faced with adversity, our emotions can be heightened, and it becomes essential to cultivate practices that promote emotional balance and support our overall well-being. Understanding the role of emotions and their impact on our lives is the first step toward effective emotional self-care. Adversity can trigger a range of emotions, including fear, sadness, anger, and frustration. These emotions are natural responses to difficult situations, but without proper management, they can lead to emotional exhaustion and mental health issues. Recognizing and addressing

## The Benefits of Emotional Self-Care

Emotional self-care helps to process and manage emotions, reducing stress and enhancing emotional resilience. It fosters a deeper understanding of oneself, promotes self-compassion, and improves overall mental health. Engaging in regular emotional self-care practices can lead to greater life satisfaction and well-being.

## Crafting Emotional Self-Care Rituals

Crafting emotional self-care rituals involves creating intentional practices that address and nurture our emotional needs. These rituals can help us process difficult emotions, foster self-compassion, and build resilience. They provide us with tools to navigate our feelings in a healthy and supportive way.

## Self-Reflection

Set aside dedicated time for self-reflection. Journaling, meditating, or engaging in reflective activities helps us explore our thoughts, feelings, and experiences. It allows us to deepen our self-awareness, gain insights, and better understand our emotional landscape.

## Journaling

Journaling is a powerful tool for self-reflection. Writing down your thoughts and feelings can help clarify emotions and provide a safe outlet for expression. Regular journaling can reveal patterns and triggers in your emotional responses, offering valuable insights for personal growth.

### Prompt Ideas for Journaling:

- What am I feeling right now?
- What events or thoughts triggered these emotions?
- How do these emotions affect my daily life and decisions?
- What steps can I take to manage these emotions healthily?

## Cultivating Mindfulness

Mindfulness plays a crucial role in emotional self-care. Being fully present in the moment, with non-judgmental awareness, helps us observe and accept our emotions without getting overwhelmed. It allows us to respond to challenging situations with greater clarity and compassion.

## Mindfulness Meditation

Mindfulness meditation involves focusing on the present moment and observing thoughts and feelings without judgment. Regular practice enhances emotional regulation, reduces stress, and improves overall well-being.

### Steps for Mindfulness Meditation:

- Find a quiet, comfortable place to sit or lie down.
- Close your eyes and take a few deep breaths.
- Focus on your breath, noticing the sensation of inhaling and exhaling.
- When your mind wanders, gently bring your focus back to your breath.
- Continue for 5-10 minutes, gradually increasing the duration as you become more comfortable with the practice.

## Expressive Arts

Engaging in expressive arts, such as painting, writing, dancing, or playing a musical instrument, can provide a powerful outlet for emotional expression. Creativity allows us to tap into our emotions, process them, and find meaning and healing through self-expression.

## Creative Practices for Emotional Expression

Painting or Drawing: Use colors and shapes to express your emotions visually. Don't worry about creating a perfect piece of art; focus on the process and how it makes you feel.

- **Writing:** Write poems, stories, or letters to express your emotions. It can be a cathartic way to release feelings and gain perspective.
- **Dancing:** Move to music that resonates with your current emotional state. Allow your body to express what words cannot.
- **Music**: Play an instrument or listen to music that reflects your emotions. Music can be a powerful tool for processing and understanding feelings.

## Seeking Therapy or Counseling

Professional support from therapists or counselors can be instrumental in emotional self-care. These professionals provide a safe space for exploring emotions, gaining insights, and developing strategies for emotional well-being.

## Benefits of Therapy

Therapy offers a structured environment to explore complex emotions and experiences. Therapists can provide valuable feedback, coping strategies, and support, helping you navigate emotional challenges more effectively.

## Types of Therapy:

- **Cognitive Behavioral Therapy (CBT):** Focuses on identifying and changing negative thought patterns and behaviors.
- **Psychodynamic Therapy**: Explores unconscious patterns and past experiences that influence current behavior.
- **Humanistic Therapy**: Emphasizes personal growth and self-actualization.
- **Mindfulness-Based Therapy:** Integrating mindfulness practices with traditional therapeutic techniques can facilitate healing.

## Establishing Boundaries

Healthy boundaries are crucial for emotional self-care. Learning to say no when necessary and limiting our time and energy prevents emotional drain. Boundaries protect our emotional well-being and foster balance in our relationships.

**Setting and Maintaining Boundaries**

- **Identify Your Needs:** Understand what you need to feel emotionally safe and healthy in your relationships and environments.
- **Communicate Clearly**: Express your boundaries assertively and respectfully. Use "I" statements to communicate your needs without blaming others.
- **Be Consistent:** Maintain your boundaries consistently. Reinforce them as needed, and don't be afraid to adjust if circumstances change.
- **Practice Self-Care:** Ensure time and space for your emotional self-care rituals. It might involve setting boundaries around work, social activities, or family obligations.

**Practicing Self-Compassion**

Cultivating self-compassion involves treating yourself with kindness, understanding, and forgiveness. Acknowledging your emotions and offering yourself empathy and support in times of difficulty is a powerful form of self-care. This practice helps build resilience and enhances emotional well-being.

**Techniques for Self-Compassion**

- **Self-Compassion Meditation:** Practice a meditation focused on self-kindness. Imagine yourself offering compassion to a friend, then extend the same kindness to yourself.
- **Affirmations**: Use positive affirmations to remind yourself of your worth and strength. Examples include "I am enough," "I am deserving of love and kindness," and "I am resilient."
- **Mindful Self-Talk:** Pay attention to your inner dialogue. When you notice negative self-talk, pause and reframe your thoughts more compassionately and supportably.

**Connecting with Others**

Developing meaningful connections is essential to emotional self-care. Reach out to trusted friends, family, or support groups. Sharing and connecting with others who understand and validate our experiences can provide immense emotional support and a sense of belonging.

**Building a Supportive Network**

- **Identify Supportive Individuals**: Reach out to people who have shown understanding and empathy. These individuals can provide emotional support and validation.

- ➤ **Join Support Groups**: Participate in groups focused on shared experiences. These groups can offer a sense of community and understanding.
- ➤ **Nurture Relationships:** Spend quality time with loved ones. Engage in activities that strengthen your connections and provide emotional nourishment.

**Additional Emotional Self-Care Practices**

There are countless ways to nurture your emotional well-being. Here are a few additional practices to consider:

### Gratitude Practice

Cultivating gratitude can shift your focus from what's lacking to what's abundant in your life. Regularly acknowledging and appreciating the positive aspects of your life can enhance emotional well-being.

- ➤ **Gratitude Journaling:** Write down three things you are grateful for each day. Reflect on the positive impact these aspects have on your life.
- ➤ **Gratitude Meditation:** Spend a few minutes each day focusing on what you are grateful for. Allow feelings of gratitude to fill your heart and mind.

**Nature Therapy**

Spending time in nature has been shown to reduce stress and improve mood. Nature therapy involves immersing yourself in natural environments to promote emotional healing.

- ➤ **Nature Walks:** Regularly walk in parks, forests, or the beach. Observe the sights, sounds, and smells of nature.
- ➤ **Gardening:** Engage in gardening activities to connect with nature. Planting, nurturing, and harvesting can be deeply therapeutic.
- ➤ **Outdoor Meditation:** Practice meditation outdoors. Find a quiet spot in nature to sit and focus on your breath and surroundings.

**Mindful Movement**

Incorporate mindful movement practices into your routine to enhance your mind-body connection and promote emotional well-being.

- ➤ **Yoga**: Practice yoga to integrate physical movement with mindfulness and breath awareness. Yoga can reduce stress, increase flexibility, and promote relaxation.

- **Tai Chi**: Engage in tai chi to improve balance, reduce stress, and cultivate inner calm.
- **Walking Meditation**: Practice walking meditation to combine physical movement with mindfulness. Focus on the sensations of walking and the rhythm of your breath.

**Moving Forward with Emotional Self-Care**

By intentionally crafting emotional self-care rituals, we nurture our emotional well-being, fostering growth, resilience, and self-compassion. These practices support us in navigating difficult emotions, building strength, and promoting overall emotional well-being.

**Integrating Emotional Self-Care into Daily Life**

- **Create a Routine**: Establish a daily or weekly routine that includes your emotional self-care practices. Consistency is critical to making these practices a regular part of your life.
- **Monitor Your Emotions**: Regularly check in with yourself to assess your emotional state. Use journaling or meditation to explore your feelings and identify areas that need attention.
- **Seek Support:** If required, don't hesitate to seek professional support. Therapists and counselors can provide valuable guidance and strategies for emotional self-care.

**Embracing Self-Compassion**

Commit to treating yourself with kindness and understanding. Practice self-compassion regularly, remind yourself it's okay to feel emotions and take time for self-care.

**Continuing the Journey**

In the final chapters, we'll explore self-care practices that focus on finding meaning and purpose in life and sustaining self-care for the long term.

## Chapter 11: Discovering Meaning and Purpose in Self-Care

This chapter will explore the importance of finding meaning and purpose in self-care and its transformative impact on personal growth. By rediscovering our values and passions through introspection, we can cultivate self-care practices that align with our meaning, leading to a more fulfilling and purpose-driven life.

### The Essence of Meaning and Purpose in Self-Care

Finding meaning and purpose in self-care is about going beyond the surface-level practices and understanding the deeper why behind the care we give ourselves. It involves reflecting on our values, what truly brings us joy and fulfillment, and aligning our self-care practices with our broader life purpose.

### The Role of Introspection

Introspection is an essential tool in this process. By taking time to reflect, journal, and engage in self-inquiry, we gain insights into our desires, dreams, and the aspects of life that truly matter to us. This introspective journey helps us rediscover our values and passions, ultimately guiding us toward meaningful self-care practices that align with our purpose.

### Techniques for Introspection

- **Journaling:** Write regularly about your thoughts, feelings, and experiences. Prompt questions can include:
  - What brings me joy and fulfillment?
  - What are my core values?
  - What activities make me feel alive and engaged?
- **Meditation**: Spend quiet contemplation, focusing on your breath and allowing thoughts to arise naturally. During this time, reflect on your values and life purpose.
- **Self-Inquiry:** Ask yourself deep questions and explore the answers without judgment. Questions might include:
  - What is my purpose in life?
  - How do I want to contribute to the world?
  - What are my long-term goals and aspirations?
  - Aligning Self-Care with Purpose

When we align our self-care practices with our purpose, it ignites a sense of satisfaction and fulfillment. It brings a more profound understanding of meaning to our experiences. It motivates us to care for ourselves in a way that nourishes our physical and emotional well-being and soul.

**Identifying Purpose-Driven Activities**

Self-care practices that align with our purpose may vary from person to person. Here are some examples of purpose-driven self-care activities:

**Volunteering and Community Engagement**

Engaging in volunteer work or community projects that resonate with your values can provide a sense of purpose and fulfillment. Whether helping at a local shelter, participating in environmental initiatives, or supporting educational programs, contributing to a cause can enrich your life and align with your purpose.

- **Steps to Get Involved:**
  - Identify causes that resonate with your values.
  - Research local organizations and opportunities.
  - Commit to a regular schedule of volunteering.
  - Reflect on the impact of your contributions and how they align with your purpose.
  - Pursuing Hobbies and Creative Outlets

Hobbies and creative activities that bring joy and self-expression are potent tools for aligning self-care with purpose. Engaging in activities like painting, writing, gardening, or playing an instrument can provide a sense of accomplishment and fulfillment.

- **Creating Space for Hobbies:**
  - Identify hobbies that bring you joy.
  - Set aside dedicated time each week for these activities.
  - Create a supportive environment for your creative pursuits.
  - Reflect on how these activities contribute to your sense of purpose and fulfillment.
  - Dedicating Time to Learning and Personal Growth

Investing in personal development through learning new skills, taking courses, or reading books that inspire you can enhance your sense of purpose. Continuous growth and learning help you stay engaged and motivated.

- **Approaches to Personal Growth:**
  - Identify areas where you want to grow or learn.
  - Enroll in classes, workshops, or online courses.
  - Dedicate time each day or week to learning.
  - Reflect on how personal growth aligns with your life purpose and goals.
  - Building Meaningful and Supportive Relationships

Nurturing relationships that support and uplift you is crucial for aligning self-care with purpose. Building a network of friends, family, and mentors who share your values and support your journey can provide emotional and spiritual nourishment.

- **Strengthening Relationships:**
  - Identify key relationships that support your values and purpose.
  - Schedule regular time to connect with these individuals.
  - Engage in meaningful conversations and activities together.
  - Reflect on how these relationships contribute to your overall purpose and well-being.
  - The Transformative Impact of Purpose-Driven Self-Care

By infusing self-care practices with a sense of purpose, we tap into a source of intrinsic motivation that fuels our growth journey. Investing in ourselves becomes a conscious choice, knowing that by doing so, we align with our deeper values and contribute to a more meaningful and fulfilling life.

**Enhanced Motivation and Commitment**

When self-care practices are purpose-driven, they become more than just routines; they become essential aspects of our lives. This alignment fosters a more profound commitment to self-care, making it easier to maintain these practices consistently.

**Greater Fulfillment and Satisfaction**

Purpose-driven self-care practices bring a profound sense of fulfillment and satisfaction. Knowing that self-care routines align with your values and life purpose can enhance your well-being and happiness.

**Increased Resilience and Strength**

Aligning self-care with purpose strengthens your resilience. When faced with challenges, you can draw on the more profound meaning and motivation behind your self-care practices to navigate adversity with greater strength and determination.

**Regularly Reassessing Your Self-Care Practices**

As you explore self-care practices that align with your purpose, remember that this is an ongoing process. Our values and passions may evolve, so it's essential to regularly check in with ourselves and reassess whether our self-care practices align with our current values and desires.

**Reflecting on Your Journey**

Set aside time periodically to reflect on your self-care journey. Consider how your practices have evolved and whether they align with your values and life purpose.

- **Reflection Questions:**
  - Are my current self-care practices aligned with my values and purpose?
  - Have my values or life purpose changed recently?
  - What adjustments can I make to align my self-care with my evolving purpose better?

**Making Adjustments**

Be open to adjusting your self-care routines as needed. As your values and life circumstances change, your self-care practices should adapt to support your growth and well-being.

- **Steps for Adjustment:**
  - Identify areas where your self-care practices need alignment.
  - Explore new activities or modify existing routines to reflect your values better.
  - Set new goals and intentions for your self-care practices.
  - Monitor the impact of these adjustments and make further changes as needed.
  - Case Studies and Personal Stories

Hearing from others who have successfully aligned their self-care practices with their purpose can provide inspiration and practical insights.

Here are a few examples:

- ➤ **Case Study: Sarah's Journey to Purpose-Driven Self-Care**

    As a marketing professional, Sarah felt unfulfilled despite her successful career. Through introspection, she realized her passion for environmental conservation. She began volunteering with local environmental groups, incorporating nature walks into her routine, and studying sustainability practices. This alignment brought her a deep sense of fulfillment and revitalized her approach to self-care.

- ➤ **Personal Story: John's Discovery of Creative Purpose**

    John, an engineer, always had a passion for painting but never made time for it. After burnout, he decided to reconnect with his creative side. He started painting regularly, joined an art community, and sold his artwork. This creative outlet renewed John's sense of purpose and significantly improved his mental and emotional well-being.

## Moving Forward with Purpose-Driven Self-Care

Integrating meaning and purpose into self-care practices creates a foundation for a more fulfilling and balanced life. This approach enhances well-being and aligns daily actions with deeper values and aspirations.

## Practical Tips for Sustaining Purpose-Driven Self-Care

- ➤ **Set Clear Intentions:** Begin each self-care activity with a clear intention that aligns with your values and purpose. This mindfulness can enhance the impact of your practices.
- ➤ **Celebrate Progress:** Acknowledge and celebrate your progress in aligning self-care with your purpose. Reflect on the positive changes and growth you have experienced.
- ➤ **Stay Open to Change:** Be willing to adapt and evolve your self-care practices as your values and life purpose change. Flexibility and openness are crucial to maintaining meaningful self-care.
- ➤ **Seek Community Support**: Engage with communities or groups that share your values and purpose. These connections can provide additional support, inspiration, and accountability.

## Embracing the Journey

Remember that discovering meaning and purpose in self-care is a continuous journey. Embrace each step, knowing your efforts contribute to a more meaningful and purpose-driven life.

In conclusion, as you explore self-care practices that align with your purpose, remember this process is unique. Regular introspection, reflection, and adaptation are essential to ensure that your self-care routines continue to support your growth and well-being.

The closing chapter will delve into sustaining self-care for long-term well-being. This chapter aims to guide us in establishing sustainable self-care routines that support our well-being and enable us to thrive. By integrating the insights and practices from this book, you can create a self-care plan that nurtures your body, mind, and spirit, leading to a life of balance, fulfillment, and purpose.

## Chapter 12: Nurturing Long-Term Self-Care for Well-Being

This closing chapter will explore strategies for sustaining self-care routines and preventing burnout. We will also highlight the importance of nurturing resilience to navigate future challenges with strength and self-compassion. Sustaining self-care is a journey that requires consistent effort and attention. It goes beyond occasional indulgences and becomes integral to our daily lives. By implementing sustainable self-care practices, we can maintain our well-being and build resilience to handle challenges.

### Establishing Sustainable Routines

### Creating Daily and Weekly Rituals

Incorporate self-care activities into daily or weekly routines. Set aside specific time slots or allocate regular intervals for self-care practices. By treating self-care as a non-negotiable part of your schedule, you make space for your well-being consistently.

- **Morning Routines**

A mindful morning routine can set a positive tone for the day. It might include:

- **Mindfulness Meditation:** Spend a few minutes in meditation to ground yourself.
- **Physical Activity**: Engage in light exercise like stretching or yoga.
- **Healthy Breakfast:** Nourish your body with a balanced meal.
- **Evening Routines**

An evening routine helps unwind and prepare for restful sleep. Consider:

- **Reflection:** Journaling about the day's experiences.
- **Relaxation:** Practices such as a warm bath or reading.
- **Sleep Hygiene:** Establishing a consistent bedtime.

### Integrating Self-Care into Daily Activities

Look for ways to weave self-care into your daily tasks. It can make it easier to maintain your routines and ensure that self-care remains a priority.

- **Mindful Commute**: Use your commute time for mindfulness practices like deep breathing or listening to calming music.

- ➤ **Work Breaks:** Take regular breaks during work to stretch, walk, or practice quick relaxation techniques.
- ➤ **Cooking:** Turn meal preparation into a mindful activity, focusing on the process and enjoying the sensory experiences.

## Prioritizing Boundaries

### Setting and Honoring Boundaries

Set clear boundaries to protect your self-care time and energy. Learn to say no to commitments or requests that do not align with your well-being. Honoring your boundaries allows you to prioritize your self-care needs without feeling guilty.

- ➤ **Identifying Boundaries**

Identify what boundaries are necessary for your well-being. It might involve:

- ❖ **Time Boundaries**: Allocating specific times for self-care.
- ❖ **Energy Boundaries**: Recognizing activities or people that drain your energy.
- ❖ **Emotional Boundaries**: Ensuring you are necessarily taking on others' emotional burdens.

- ➤ **Communicating Boundaries**

Effectively communicate your boundaries to others. Use "I" statements to express your needs clearly and assertively:

- ❖ "I need some time alone after work to recharge."
- ❖ "I appreciate your invitation, but I must prioritize self-care this evening."

## Continual Learning

### Staying Open to New Practices

Stay open to learning and adapting self-care practices. Explore new techniques, activities, or modalities that resonate with you and incorporate them into your routine. Engaging in lifelong learning helps keep your self-care practices fresh and inspiring.

- ➤ **Exploring Different Modalities**

Try various self-care modalities to discover what works best for you:

- ❖ **Therapies:** Experiment with different types of treatment, such as cognitive-behavioral therapy, art therapy, or acupuncture.
- ❖ **Workshops and Classes**: Attend seminars or classes on self-care practices like mindfulness, yoga, or nutrition.
- ❖ **Reading and Research:** Read books and articles on self-care to gain new insights and ideas.

➢ **Reflecting on Learning**

Reflect on what you learn and how it impacts your self-care routine regularly. This can help you integrate new practices more effectively and stay motivated to continue your self-care journey.

- ❖ **Questions for Reflection:**
  - What new self-care practices have I discovered recently?
  - How have these practices benefited my well-being?
  - Are there any practices that did not resonate with me, and why?

## Practicing Self-Compassion

### Being Kind to Yourself

Be kind and compassionate toward yourself as you navigate your self-care journey. Understand that self-care is not about perfection or achieving unrealistic expectations. Give yourself permission to rest, recharge, and make mistakes. Self-compassion sustains your motivation and guards against burnout.

### Techniques for Self-Compassion

- ➢ **Self-Compassion Meditation:** Practice meditation focused on self-kindness and understanding. Imagine yourself offering compassion to a friend, then extend the same kindness to yourself.
- ➢ **Positive Affirmations**: Use affirmations to reinforce a compassionate mindset. Examples include "I am worthy of self-care," "I forgive myself for my mistakes," and "I am doing my best."

### Allowing Yourself to Rest

Rest is a critical component of self-care. Allow yourself to take breaks and rest without guilt. Recognize that rest is essential for overall well-being and productivity.

### Regular Evaluation

#### Assessing Your Self-Care Routine

Regularly evaluate the effectiveness of your self-care routines and adjust as needed. Reflect on what practices are serving you well and bringing you joy, and let go of those that no longer resonate. Stay attuned to changes in your needs and modify your self-care routines accordingly.

- **Tools for Evaluation**
  - **Journaling:** Keep a self-care journal to track your activities and their impact on your well-being. Reflect on what practices have been most beneficial.
  - **Self-Check-Ins:** Schedule regular self-check-ins to assess your physical, emotional, and mental health and identify areas that need more attention.

### Adapting to Change

Be flexible and willing to adapt your self-care practices as your circumstances and needs change. Life is dynamic, and your self-care routine should evolve to support you through distinct phases and challenges.

#### Building Supportive Networks

### Cultivating Relationships

Surround yourself with individuals who support and encourage your self-care journey. Cultivate relationships with people who understand the importance of prioritizing well-being and can provide support and accountability. Share your self-care goals with loved ones to foster a supportive network.

### Finding Supportive Communities

- **Support Groups**: Join groups focused on self-care, wellness, or specific interests that resonate with you.
- **Social Networks**: Use social media to connect with like-minded individuals and communities.
- **Mentorship**: Seek mentors who can guide and support your self-care journey.

### Maintaining Supportive Relationships

Regularly engage with your supportive network to maintain strong connections. It might include:

- ➢ Regular Check-Ins: Schedule regular check-ins with friends or family to discuss your self-care goals and progress.
- ➢ Shared Activities: Participate in self-care activities, such as group workouts, cooking healthy meals, or attending wellness workshops.

## Nurturing Resilience

**Developing Resilience**

Develop resilience to navigate future challenges with strength. Resilience involves cultivating a positive mindset, embracing uncertainty, seeking support, and practicing self-compassion. Through resilience, you bounce back from setbacks, learn from difficulties, and adapt gracefully to change.

**Techniques for Building Resilience**

- ➢ **Positive Thinking**: Practice positive thinking to reframe challenges as opportunities for growth. Focus on what you can learn from demanding situations.
- ➢ **Embracing Uncertainty**: Accept that uncertainty is a part of life. Develop flexibility and adaptability to navigate unexpected changes.
- ➢ **Seeking Support**: Reach out for support when needed. Lean on your supportive network and seek professional help if necessary.

## Practicing Self-Compassion

Self-compassion is a critical component of resilience. Treat yourself with kindness and understanding during tough times. Recognize that setbacks and difficulties are a natural part of life.

- ➢ **Self-Compassion Exercises:** Engage in exercises that promote self-compassion, such as loving-kindness meditation or writing a compassionate letter to yourself.
  - ❖ Practical Tips for Sustaining Long-Term Self-Care
  - ❖ Creating a Self-Care Plan
  - ❖ Develop a comprehensive self-care plan that outlines your goals, routines, and strategies for sustaining self-care over the long term.

**Steps to Create a Self-Care Plan:**
- ➢ **Identify Goals:** Define your self-care goals and what you hope to achieve.
- ➢ **Outline Routines:** Create daily, weekly, and monthly routines that incorporate your self-care practices.

- ➤ **Set Milestones**: Establish milestones to track your progress and celebrate achievements.
- ➤ **Evaluate and Adjust:** Regularly review your self-care plan and adjust as needed.

## Embracing Flexibility

Be flexible with your self-care routines. Understand that your needs and circumstances may change, and your self-care practices should adapt accordingly.

**Tips for Flexibility:**

- ➤ **Regular Reflection:** Regularly reflect on your self-care practices and adjust as needed.
- ➤ **Open-Mindedness:** Stay open to trying new self-care techniques and activities.
- ➤ **Adapting to Change**: Embrace change as an opportunity to gain experience and evolve your self-care practices.

**Integrating Self-Care into All Aspects of Life**

Incorporate self-care into all areas of your life, including work, relationships, and leisure activities. This holistic approach ensures that self-care becomes a natural and integral part of your daily routine.

- ➤ **Work-Life Balance:** Maintain a healthy balance between work and personal life. Set boundaries to protect your time and prioritize self-care.
- ➤ **Healthy Relationships:** Foster relationships that will support your well-being. Surround yourself with individuals who encourage and uplift you.
- ➤ **Leisure Activities:** Engage in leisure activities that bring joy and relaxation. Make time for hobbies and interests that nourish your soul.

## The Role of Self-Care in Preventing Burnout

**Recognizing Signs of Burnout**

Understand the signs of burnout, including physical exhaustion, emotional fatigue, decreased motivation, and a sense of detachment. Recognizing these signs early will help you take proactive steps to prevent burnout.

**Signs of Burnout:**

- **Physical Symptoms**: Chronic fatigue, headaches, or sleep disturbances.
- **Emotional Symptoms**: Irritability, anxiety, or feelings of hopelessness.
- **Behavioral** symptoms include reduced performance and productivity, increased absenteeism, withdrawal from responsibilities, isolation, distancing oneself from colleagues, friends, and family, and avoiding social interactions. Procrastination, Changes in Eating Habits Substance Use: Neglecting Self-Care, and Sleep Problems

# Conclusion

In this journey towards sustained self-care, remember that the steps you take are not acts of selfishness but rather essential measures for nurturing your overall health and happiness. By embracing self-care, you are equipping yourself to be the best version for your benefit and those around you. It enables you to face life's challenges with greater strength, resilience, and deep self-compassion. Self-care is more than just a series of actions or practices; it is a mindset and a way of life. It is about recognizing your worth and the necessity of taking care of yourself to maintain physical, emotional, and mental health. Self-care is an ongoing journey that evolves with your changing needs and circumstances.

One of the most crucial aspects to understand is that self-care is not selfish. Taking time to care for yourself ensures you have the energy and emotional capacity to care for others. It prevents burnout and promotes a sustainable way of living that benefits everyone around you. Practicing self-care regularly builds resilience. Life's challenges are inevitable, but with a strong foundation of self-care, you can face these challenges with more extraordinary fortitude and grace. Resilience is about bouncing back from adversity and growing more robust and capable with each experience. Your path to self-care is one of continuous exploration and adaptation. As life evolves, so should your self-care practices. Be open to discovering new ways to nurture yourself, and be willing to adjust your strategies as your needs change. This flexibility is critical to maintaining a balanced and fulfilling life.

Life is dynamic, and your self-care practices must be adaptable. Whether you are experiencing a significant life change like a new job, a move, or a personal change, your self-care routine should reflect these changes to support you effectively. Stay curious and open-minded about new self-care practices. What works for you today might not be as effective tomorrow, and that's okay. Embrace new activities, techniques, and approaches that resonate with you and contribute to your well-being.

Your dedication to this path is a significant investment in your well-being. This commitment speaks volumes about your desire to live a harmonious and balanced life. As you progress on this journey, may this book serve as a steadfast companion and guide, offering insights and encouragement at every step. Take time regularly to assess your self-care practices and their impact on your life. Reflect on what is working well and what might need adjustment. This ongoing self-assessment ensures that your self-care routine remains effective and aligned with your current needs. Acknowledge and celebrate your progress along the way. Every step you take towards better self-care is a victory. Celebrating these milestones reinforces your commitment and motivates you to prioritize your well-being.

In closing, we wish you a path filled with growth, resilience, and well-being. May you continue to flourish and thrive in all areas of your life, always remembering the importance of nurturing yourself. Your self-care journey is a beautiful testament to your commitment to living a life of balance and happiness. As you nurture yourself, you will find that you flourish in all areas of life—personal, professional, and social. Self-care enhances your ability to enjoy life, achieve goals, and maintain meaningful relationships. The benefits of self-care extend beyond yourself. When you are well-cared for, you can more effectively care for others. Your well-being positively impacts those around you, creating a ripple effect of health and happiness.

Remember that self-care is a lifelong journey. There will be ups and downs, moments of significant progress, and times when it feels challenging. Stay committed to yourself, and keep moving forward, knowing that every effort you make towards self-care is a step towards a more balanced, fulfilling life.

Dear Reader,

As you hold this book, thank you for embarking on this journey with me. Your decision to explore these pages is not just about reading another book; it's about joining a shared journey of discovery and growth.

Writing this book has been a voyage of deep reflection and learning, and I am thrilled to share it with you. Each chapter is infused with the essence of experiences, insights, and realizations that have shaped my understanding of what it truly means to nurture oneself.

As you read through these pages, I hope you find moments that resonate with you, words that challenge you, and ideas that inspire you to explore new dimensions of your life. This book is not just a narration of thoughts but an invitation for you to reflect, question, and perhaps even find new pathways to your well-being.

Your engagement with this book completes its purpose. I sincerely hope it is a valuable companion in your journey, illuminating paths and opening doors to new possibilities.

Thank you for your time, openness, and willingness to journey with me through these pages. May this book be a source of comfort, insight, and inspiration as you navigate the beautiful complexity of your life.

With gratitude and best wishes,

*Tracy A. Allen*

# Books By This Author

## My Truth: A Lady's Secret's A Woman's Confessions

Every person has secrets. Some that are dark, some that may be dirty, and some that we may even take to our graves. Some secrets are so devastating that they can destroy one's life or drive one insane. I believe that everyone has a secret or two. Instead, it is big or small; if no one knows about it but you, it is a secret. The secret is a term that has been a part of my life for so long. It is a term that I'm sure that everyone can relate to. It was part of my conception, my growing up, my marriage, and my career; it was law in my home growing up. "Do not ever tell what was going on in the home or behind closed doors." was the motto. It was a term that a lady doesn't kiss and tell. We all have our secrets. If we were to share them, I am sure that most of us would be so ashamed that we probably would do something so drastic as to hide the embarrassment, to the point that we might go into hiding afterward or even worse. So, that is the reason for this book: to CONFESS my SECRETS so that you too can see into my world of heartache, pain, and deception as I bare it all for you to see.

## Children's Book Series First in its serious

## "Roxie and Rosco's Adventures: Lessons in Loyalty, Truth, and Honesty"

Welcome to a small, cozy house at the end of a quiet cul-de-sac. With its inviting porch and cheerful flower boxes, this charming home exudes warmth and comfort. However, the real magic lies just beyond the back door, where a large backyard stretches out, teeming with life and adventure. It is where the heart of our story beats, for it is the domain of two very special Pitbulls, Roxie and Rosco. Together, Roxie and Rosco form an inseparable duo. Their days are filled with playful romps through the backyard, lazy afternoons basking in the sun, and quiet evenings curled by the fireplace. Their bond is unbreakable, built on mutual respect and unwavering loyalty. As you enter their world, you'll discover the magic in everyday moments. The adventures they embark on, the lessons they learn, and the love they share will warm your heart and remind you of life's simple joys. So, join Roxie and Rosco in their cozy home with a large backyard. There's always room for one more in their endless possibilities and boundless love.

# About the Author

Dr. Tracy A. Allen is a proud mother of two grown sons, Jerome Antonio Johnson II and Travis Boaz Johnson. As a retired Army Officer who served for 20 years, Tracy has traveled the globe due to her military career, receiving numerous accolades for her professionalism, leadership, and dedication to her country. Among her many honors, she received the Bronze Star for her exceptional governance and proficiency.

Tracy holds a Bachelor of Science Degree in Psychology, a Master of Arts in Mental Health Professional Counseling, a Master of Science in Mental Health Professional Counseling, and a PhD in Professional Counseling.

After retiring from the military, Tracy has made significant contributions in various fields. She has worked in Information Assurance for Intcon, Logistics for Dimensions/Honeywell, the Defense Intelligence Agency (DIA), as a Therapist for Premier Behavioral and New Beginnings, and as a College Career and Human Resources Instructor at Fayetteville Technical Community College. Now, a business owner and CEO of Allen Consulting Firm, LLC & TrayLuxe Desing.

Tracy is actively involved in her community and professional organizations., the National Association of Professional Women, the American Counseling Association, the American Psychological Association, the International Association of Marriage and Family Counselors, the National Geographic Society, the American Mental Health Counselors Association, the Institute of Community Leadership, and a member of the Fayetteville Chambers of Commerce. She is also a dedicated member of Simon Temple AME Zion Church and the Alpha Kappa Alpha Sorority, Incorporated Upsilon Kappa Omega Chapter of Fayetteville, Fort Liberty, and Pope Air Force Base, NC.

Dr Tracy A. Allen's life and career reflect her unwavering commitment to service, education, and community.

"Nurturing Self-Care:

Empowering Resilience through Life's Challenges."

By Dr. Tracy A. Allen

Made in the USA
Columbia, SC
10 September 2024